.

THE BRIDGE TO BETTER

THE SMALL BUSINESS LEADER'S BLUEPRINT FOR REIGNITING GROWTH

5 PROVEN STEPS TO CLOSE THE GAP BETWEEN CURRENT AND BEST PERFORMANCE

JESSICA V. WEATHERFORD

WITH CONTRIBUTION BY
NEAL M. BOTTOM

Acknowledgements

We first and foremost owe a huge amount of gratitude to our incredible clients and colleagues who have, over the years, invited us into their businesses and lives to support their growth and leadership. In addition, only through the patience and constant support of our families would we have been able to found our consulting firm, write this book, and push our own boundaries of learning, growth and leadership.

We'd also like to specifically thank Peter Michaels, David Green and Larry Peck for the time spent sharing their stories and wholeheartedly supporting this project. Each of them elicits the best from those around them, which is exactly the type leadership we hope to inspire with this book.

Table of Contents

Introduction

You purchased this book for one or more of the following reasons:

1. Your organization is in a growth funk.

2. Your teams can't seem to get it together enough to achieve their goals.

3. You are concerned that your organization has grown faster than your management skills can keep up with.

First, it's important to note that you are not alone. This is actually a very common, and very important, time in the growth of a small business or non-profit. It is one of the many obstacles you will experience on your leadership journey, and your ability to overcome it will determine whether your organization regains a positive trajectory or continues into a vicious downward spiral.

We know you've sought the antidote to this problem elsewhere: sitting through the seminars, attending conferences and reading all those team performance blog posts that fill your email inbox. Yet you're still fighting the same frustrating battle to transform your team into the league of superheroes you know they could be. We know you've seen a month or so of shining performance when you've tried something new, but for some reason the results never last. The new level of performance just doesn't stick.

This book is the antidote to your frustration. By the end of the book, you will have taken your management mastery to a new level, empowering you with the ability to once again kickstart the engine of growth within your organization. Neal and I wrote this book specifically to empower you to bridge the gap between your team's current and best performance, as well as ensure you are able to empower them to *sustain* that best performance. The best product or service in the world cannot reach its target customers when the team providing it is in disarray, experiencing toxic interactions and working out of alignment with each other. In these pages you will find success stories, hard data, and practical, applicable tools you and your team can begin using immediately to bring your team back to a place of alignment, growth and high-performance.

You are working in a very exciting time. This book could not have been written ten years ago. Over the past decade, scholars have been hard at work identifying how your team can increase its efficiency, agility, and profitability. Research has focused so intensely on the dynamics of powerful teams that it's no longer a question of *how* a team can reach its full potential, but *when*.

What in the past might have seemed like team magic or perfect chemistry we can now clearly define and put into daily practice. This book distills this priceless team performance research into five easily digestible key elements that will help you take your team, and your organization, to a whole new level: Laying your team's foundation, defining and increasing organizational performance, sparking and sustaining improved individual performance, ensuring peak team performance, and, finally, developing and sustaining improved leadership performance. We end with tips for ensuring your team is what's known as a *learning team*, or a team that is continuously seeking to improve itself. In a nutshell, we drank more coffee than we care to admit in order to scour thousands of pages of academic findings so you don't have to.

What took us years to gather will take you only weeks to read and begin to implement. This book will also provide you with best practices for managing the changes once they are implemented and with steps for continuing to build on the positive growth you experience.

Like best practices picked up at a conference, it's going to be extremely tempting to latch onto one or two of the key elements we share with you as the magic bullet. Resist the reductionist urge! Think of these five elements as equally important parts of your bridge to better. If one is missing, the bridge may seem like progress, but won't actually see your team across to growth. Each of the five elements serves a different purpose; together, they lead to your team's best performance.

That does not mean, however, that you need to implement every one of these five elements *at the same time.* As we take a look at how the brain responds to change, it will become apparent why tackling one element at a time is a better course of action.

Part I

Preparing for Growth

Chapter 1

The First Three Steps

While writing this book, it was impossible for us not to remember what horrible team leaders we were at the start of our careers. We were both passionate about the continuous improvement needed for long-term success, but like many ambitious young professionals, we thought that the best team performance resulted from an aggressive, commanding leadership style. If you've ever tried this method of leadership, you are familiar with the responses we received: defensiveness, decreased motivation, and, in some of the worst cases, literally seeing the light in people's eyes die as they tune you out.

As young leaders, we both had a talent for looking at a system and seeing the opportunities for improvement. Within days of being assigned to a project or team, we could point out the specific processes that needed redesigning or the individuals that needed motivating.

Back then, we didn't hesitate to make our observations known immediately or to push our team members to change just as quickly. Many of our clients who take this same approach to change get exactly the same results we got: paltry improvements. In addition to being disappointing, the improvements tended to disappear just as quickly as they appeared when team members fell right back into their old comfort zones.

Neither of us could figure out why our intelligent, ambitious teams couldn't seem to get on board with any real improvement. Well, we're happy to report we now know exactly why. And our previous teams will be happy to read that the fault was entirely ours.

We went wrong by assuming that our team members would see and accept our concerns as theirs. We made the mistake of calling on our teams to act and improve while they still valued the status quo as the best they had to offer. This put our teams on the defensive instead of giving them the opportunity to pursue a shared vision.

As with many teams not yet giving their best, productivity, revenues, and profits were always good enough to support the status quo. Why shake things up when we're doing "all right"? At the time, we as leaders knew that "all right" would only last so long, but we didn't always know how to communicate that message.

You know this, too. You know that "all right" will not get you, your team, or your organization the great achievements you are working so hard for. You want your team to jump the gap between current performance and the *best* performance. We are going to get you there.

A Marathon, Not a Sprint

It is important to keep in mind, however, that the myth of overnight team perfection is not unlike the myth of the overnight sensation. Malcolm Gladwell dispelled both of these myths eloquently in his bestseller *Outliers*.[1] Gladwell used the Beatles as an example of a wild success that at first glance seemed to come with ease and immediacy. In actuality, as Gladwell points out, The Ed Sullivan Show and throngs of screaming fans were preceded by years of dedicated practice and constant calibration.

As you take your team to its highest level of performance, you will need similar focus, dedication, and patience. The best leaders often make high performance seem effortless, but don't be fooled. Every piece of research and every case study we share tell a story of constant discipline and focus. Of course, after enough practice, you, like the Beatles, will make reaching higher and higher levels of success look effortless.

Along the way you will be tempted to give up on your new practices. Co-executives, staff members and even business partners might challenge you. When this happens, you may feel your resolve start to wane. It will be critical to ask yourself one question: *What is at stake if we don't change?*

For many of our clients, not changing means decreasing revenues, higher turnover, and lost cash flow. These symptoms can only be endured for so long. Left unmitigated, each can spell the end of an entire company.

Think about mastery you have sought in your life. It might be mastery of an instrument, a sport, or even leadership. When you first began applying your energy to playing guitar, you felt clumsy, cautious, and utterly without talent. After months of fundamentals, you were able to work in some nuance. After a couple of years, you had your own style. The fundamentals don't even register as intentional action in your brain any longer. They are now habitual, and you have the knowledge, experience, and skills to take performances to an even higher level.

You must approach the lessons in this book in the exact same way. You *will* at times feel clumsy. You *will* hope a conversation goes better next time. You *will* be frustrated that it's not easy right away. And most importantly, you *will* be far out of your comfort zone.

But what do we know happens when we step out of our comfort zone? Growth. Achievement. Innovation. If you as a leader stay safe within your comfort zone, your team will stay there as well. The comfort zone habit brings us right back to a team that rests happily in status quo, with slowly eroding revenues and profits chipping away at organizational success and job security. A team or business that fights to maintain the status quo will find itself floundering as the marketplace changes rapidly around it. The status quo is unsustainable over the long term, and eventually the work suffers, which can lead to the end of a small business or team entirely.

When you refuse to succumb to a slow team death via the status quo, you are committing to continuous improvement. To be successful over the long term, an organization must continuously adapt, innovate, and grow. This means that teams must continuously adapt, innovate, and grow. And for teams to continuously improve, guess who else has to continuously improve? Yep—*you*. Every member of the team is responsible for growing and adapting, which means constantly pushing the edge of the comfort zone.

Seeking to master the guitar, a triathlon, or team leadership is not easy. Discipline is key—discipline is what separates the Beatles from the bands you've never heard of.

Team underperformance can mean literally millions of lost potential profits in a small business or non-profit. Dysfunctional teams and broken systems can produce acceptable results for only so long. Since we have a high degree of labor movement in our country, top performers are a scarce resource—demand far outpaces supply. You can help shape high performers, which is one of this book's main topics, but you will not attract or retain ambitious, growth-oriented individuals if they experience a critical mass of inefficient processes and disappointingly dysfunctional culture right away. An organization that cannot attract or retain new recruits will begin to contract as managers retire, beginning a downward spiral that decreases revenue and profits.

Read the below advice and remember it. Write it on a sticky note and stick it on your computer. Make it your screensaver. Whatever you do, never, *ever* forget:

Building team buy-in for change is the first and most crucial step in taking a team to its best performance.

If you read this and said "Duh!" out loud or rolled your eyes at the sheer simplicity of it, pause for a second. Think about how many leaders you know who fail to take the time and ensure they have genuine buy-in. We know you can name lots of them. We can name lots of them. Because, *almost nobody takes the time to build the buy-in.*

Yes, it's simple. The difference between mediocrity and greatness is often simply the discipline and effort that goes into the simple things. Great leaders with high-performing teams take the time to build a strong foundation for change before ever asking their teams to improve.

Before you can get back to growth, buy-in *must* be present. If you want to get past the defensiveness, the frustration, and the dead stare of indifference, these next steps will get you there.

Eight Steps to Change

Now, let's take a look at the best way to elicit your team's buy-in. For guidance, we turn to John Kotter, a professor of leadership and change at Harvard Business School and an expert on change management. Kotter has an elegant eight-step model that we leverage with every team and organizational transformation.

1. Establish a sense of urgency
2. Create a guiding coalition
3. Develop a change vision
4. Communicate the vision for buy-in
5. Empower broad-based action
6. Generate short-term wins
7. Never let up
8. Incorporate the changes into the culture

We strongly encourage you to read more about each of these steps in Kotter's excellent book, *Leading Change.*[2] In our work, we have found time and again that the first three steps are the crucial ones for building a solid foundation for any performance improvement effort. As we outline how you can prepare to take your team to the next level, we will be focusing on

1. Establishing a sense of urgency

2. Creating a guiding coalition

3. Developing a change vision

Early in our work, we underestimated the importance of the first three steps to building a strong foundation and watched as team members struggled to make the performance improvements they were seeking. Just as when we were young leaders, some change efforts were stopped dead in their tracks while some never reached their potential because they were operating on shaky ground to begin with. Don't make that mistake! Ensure you have spent ample time creating the best possible start to your effort by focusing first on each of the three steps.

Step 1: A Sense of Urgency

First and foremost, a team must share a sense of urgency leading to a desire to change. Many have called this sense "the burning platform." The team has no choice but to jump into new behaviors because the current way of doing things is burning to the ground.

Resistance to change comes down to biology. Our brains are not wired to welcome change; in fact, our brains and body seek comfortable *stasis*. Essentially, once our basic needs are met and we find a certain level of fulfillment within any situation, our brains will work to maintain the status quo. Your brain seeks comfort and survival first and foremost. By creating emotional resistance to change, your brain is asking you, "We eat well, we have a roof over our head, and we have some pretty good relationships, why do we need to change?"

Let us introduce your brain's gatekeepers of change: the basal ganglia and the amygdala. The basal ganglia are the part of the brain that establish patterns and allow you to develop habits (walking, driving, closing deals in a certain way). The more often you repeat the habit, the stronger the neural links within the basal ganglia become. This means that to be open to change, your brain has to physically fight the urge to rely on those already-forged links. In their 2011 article "That's the Way We (Used To) Do Things Around Here," Schwartz, Gaito, and Lennick argue that "if you want to create permanent new patterns of behavior in people (including yourself), you must embed [the new patterns] in the basal ganglia. Taking on new patterns (also known as learning) often feels unfamiliar and painful, because it means consciously overriding deeply comfortable neuronal circuitry."[3]

The amygdala is your brain's emotional center, and it's no wallflower in this process. As you are inspiring your team members to aspire to a new level of growth via improvements in their ways of work, their basal ganglia are recognizing that this means letting go of habits, which triggers the amygdala to launch a potential emotional hijacking. This happens because the brain wants to stick with its comfortable habits, and asking it to move out of its well-worn groove results in the resistance you encounter when you lead a change effort. Symptoms of the amygdala's hijacking include anger, fear, defensiveness, and embarrassing outbursts that make the HR department very nervous.

Here's the bad news: Improvement *is* change. That means that as you work to lead an improvement effort, you are essentially leading a change effort. In other words, you are working against millions of years of evolutionary biology as you work to inspire individuals to reject stasis and strive for something greater. Don't put the book down yet. There is some good news, too.

Here it is—the good news: First, by communicating a sense of urgency, you are showing your team that stasis—their comfort zone, their well-worn groove—is actually under threat. Once individuals share a sense of urgency, they can all recognize that their comfort and success are dependent on continuous performance improvement. When prehistoric humans recognized that their prey was becoming scarce, they were more open to breaking habits and moving somewhere with more plentiful prey. Our brains are not very different than those of our distant ancestors. It's up to you as the change leader to create a sense of scarcity, opening up the brain to the possibility of change and new habits.

Wait, there's even more good news: Learning to improve is a skill, and, like any skill, it can be practiced and mastered. According to Schwartz, Gaito, and Lennick, "despite the seeming inflexibility of the brain, neural connections are highly plastic; even the most entrenched thought patterns can be changed."[4] Think about any type of physical activity you improved at over time. At first you felt clumsy and awkward when you practiced, but with discipline and support, your confidence grew and the movements began to feel natural.

A team seeking to improve performance is no different. At first, the conversations that are needed in order to identify changes and confront obstacles will feel foreign and frustrating. The brain will intercept and say "Hey! Remember when we were happy and comfortable in our status quo?" That voice will get weaker and weaker over time as the team becomes accustomed to changing, growing, and learning new, more effective ways of behaving. Interestingly, once the brain stops interpreting change as a threat and instead interprets it as a habit, it will raise resistance less and less often.

Light a Fire under Your Team

Think about your current sense of urgency. Your desire for growth and profitability is present every day, raising red flags in your brain and screaming for you to change this status quo before it's too late. Specifically, your sense of urgency might include

- Fear that unless your team begins to embrace new systems and behaviors, they won't be able to achieve the level of revenue and profit needed for long-term viability.

- The recognition that your organization is wasting hundreds of thousands of dollars on recruiting new employees that it can't retain.

- Acknowledgement that valuing organizational tradition and best practices has evolved into dangerous protectionism that threatens the long-term bottom line.

Remember, however, that your team must share in this sense of urgency. There is one more thing about the brain you ought to know. In its struggle to resist the stress of constant change and to hold onto stasis, the brain actively rejects new ideas (even facts) that contradict what it currently believes is true. How did the world react when Galileo supported Copernicus's findings that the Earth revolved around the Sun? Not exactly with open arms.

Long ago, before we knew to elicit strong buy-in prior to undertaking significant changes, when our teams heard that their behaviors and processes were eroding profits and leading to the company's long-term demise, it went against everything they believed to be true about their actions within the company. Biology ensured that we didn't have a snowball's chance in hell of uniting the team around this issue without first creating a shared sense of urgency.

In *Leading Change*, Kotter explains that "sooner or later, no matter how hard [leaders] push, no matter how hard they threaten, if many others don't feel the same sense of urgency, the momentum for change will probably die far short of the finish line. People will find a thousand ways to withhold cooperation from a process that they sincerely think is unnecessary or wrongheaded."[5] So, what specific tactics can you employ to build buy-in before asking your team to reach for their best performance?

The first step to building a sense of urgency is identifying like minds. Creating a sense of urgency means building a critical mass, so identifying the person on the team most likely to share your concern is the first step. Continuing to share your sense of urgency and the reasons for it, in formal one-on-one meetings or informally over coffee, will also get the upward spiral moving. An initial change in a status-quo-favoring environment almost always requires a sense of urgency. However, as your team becomes higher performing and more innovative, the momentum for healthy change and improvement increases and even becomes self-sustaining because team members recognize opportunities for greater efficiency, effectiveness, and growth.

It's critical to know what the person you are talking to cares most about. If you're sharing some of these ideas with a co-executive or staff member in a one-on-one format, it's important to understand whether they cares more about the bottom line or more about culture. If your colleague cares most about the bottom line, then you can present a calculation and share your concern about future profits. If they work hardest at creating a positive culture, then you should tailor the discussion around whether or not certain aspects of the culture are living up to their hopes and expectations.

Your team approach should be similar. Almost every team we have worked with is self-aware enough to recognize that they aren't working together at their *best.* When we work on building a sense of urgency, we elicit from the team what their concerns are. We sometimes ask, "If this team or company were to fail, what would be the leading factors in its demise?"

Getting both leadership and the team to share the sense of a burning platform prepares them to leap toward higher achievement.

Checklist for Creating a Sense of Urgency

- You can clearly identify specific threats to team or organizational success.
- You can describe the financial consequences of failing to improve.
- You can describe nonfinancial consequences of failing to improve.

- You have begun having discussions with individuals around your concerns and are building a critical mass of support.

Step 2: Build a Guiding Coalition

Once you have built a critical mass around a shared sense of urgency, it's time to gather the coalition of champions that will see the change through.

How do you know when you have enough support to put together a guiding coalition to shepherd the change through? These three things will have occurred:

1. All executives and a majority of staff agree that change must occur for success to be sustainable.

2. The number of team members who share the sense of urgency equals the number of people needed to actually do the work to bring about change.

3. The team members on board with seeing a change through have enough authority to prevent major internal obstacles to the implementation process.

We cannot stress this enough: If the organization's team of executives does not fully share the sense of urgency, the change effort is imperiled from the beginning. The executives control which resources controlled by them are devoted to which priorities; if the executive does not see the necessary change as a priority, then he or she will not allocate the resources (time, people, money) needed to bring about the change.

The executive should not only share in the sense of urgency, but should absolutely be a part of the guiding coalition. Imagine trying to improve the performance of a baseball team without the support or presence of the coaches. If the players tried to initiate a performance improvement plan without the buy-in and participation of coaches, any coach left out would very likely become defensive, ensuring the performance improvement plan would stop dead in its tracks. As a champion of change, you need the all the leaders on board.

With the executives on board, it's now time to form the guiding coalition. It's been our experience that seven people or fewer are best for creating and executing plans, and that a larger number leaves a team spinning its wheels in the mud. Too large a group, and there are either too many disparate voices to agree on a direction or group think emerges, which prevents critical dissent from informing the best decisions.

If the performance improvement effort you are embarking on spans multiple departments and hundreds of employees, we recommend a cross-functional guiding coalition that ensures multiple perspectives on the organization. From the guiding coalition, each function can have a separate group tasked with executing the improvement tactics appropriate for that particular function.

One final and critical component that the guiding coalition must consider is bandwidth. We define *bandwidth* as the time and energy available to devote to new initiatives in addition to daily job responsibilities. We have consulted with guiding coalitions that have little to no bandwidth, which has meant that all the work we've done together never gets implemented or practiced because there is just not enough time in the day to manage organizational priorities and work on performance improve-ment.

Here's a hint: If during the guiding coalition recruitment process you find that potential members are hesitant to join the coalition because they aren't sure they will have the time to devote to it, listen to them. We find this type of red flag early in the process must be heeded, or it leads to disappointing bottlenecks and frustration down the road.

Any team performance improvement effort requires at least a couple hours per week for planning, execution, practice, and feedback. If this time commitment is a problem for potential coalition members, it doesn't mean they shouldn't be a part of the effort. It *does* mean that their responsibilities and schedule need to be addressed before they join. All members of the guiding coalition need to have those two hours per week (and early in the process, sometimes more) available before they commit to the coalition.

Code of Conduct

Once the guiding coalition is assembled, we always spend the first meeting setting a coalition code of conduct. What are the five to ten behaviors that will keep this group performing highly itself? Examples of these behaviors include:

- Arriving on time and prepared
- Offering positive feedback early and often
- Seeking information for decision-making
- Verifying with data or qualifying any assumptions
- Preparing projects in a way that results in customer delight
- Returning calls and emails within forty-eight business hours
- Minding the ABC: Always Be Curious

The code of conduct helps keep the guiding coalition on track and also sets the stage for accountability, which will be a crucial component of your performance improvement effort.

Okay, you are now two-thirds of the way to being prepared to begin your team performance improvement effort. You have identified a pressing sense of urgency and created a guiding coalition whose members have both the desire and the authority to plan and drive change throughout the team.

Charter

A team charter is an absolute necessity for defining what this team will do, how it will do it and how long it will take. Without a charter, the team will find itself spinning its wheels in the mud...lots of power at the table but going nowhere.

A team charter can consist of many different elements, and you should feel free to customize it according to the team's needs. We often recommend that it include a minimum of objectives, assumptions, deliverables, timeframe, the project management approach and the reporting structure for decision-making.

You'll note throughout this book that we recommend applying the art of definition to your organization's strategy, goals, projects, teams, etc. As an organization matures, definition is necessary to keep staff (and executives!) on the same page. What takes a minor investment of time up-front results in major savings through the efficient and effective alignment of people with growth.

Checklist for Building the Guiding Coalition

- You have recruited enough team members to the guiding coalition to ensure sufficient support for discussion, planning, and implementation.

- The authority of the guiding coalition is strong enough to prevent major internal obstacles.

- You have ensured that the coalition has the bandwidth to manage the performance improvement effort.

- The guiding coalition has created a code of conduct that outlines how it will function to ensure success.

- The guiding coalition has created a team charter.

Step 3: Developing a Change Vision

"Vision," according to Kotter, "refers to a picture of the future with some implicit or explicit commentary on why people should strive to create that future."[6]

Why is a shared change vision so critical to change success? For the same reason that knowing your destination is important when you're travelling—so you don't waste precious time and money drifting aimlessly here and there. Your team isn't interested in aimless drifting; your team is interested in improving to resume growth. By identifying the vision up front, you are able to plan the necessary steps to reach it as well as allocate the resources necessary to get you there.

On a team of individuals with wildly different perspectives, experiences, and functions, different people will bring their own luggage filled with desired outcomes. Creating a shared change vision early in the process ensures that all those desired outcomes are on the table and have the chance to be taken into consideration. The change vision may not include every desired outcome, but inviting the discussion secures a much higher level of buy-in from all guiding coalition participants.

A shared vision creates alignment out of the gate. The team may have varying opinions about *how* to best improve performance, but exactly *what* performance improvements are expected will be clear to each and every individual.

As Kotter mentioned, the vision should include the *why* as well. Why is the *why* important? Six months into the performance improvement effort, when the team has met resistance, spent hours on bottlenecks and processes, and maybe wants to quit the whole damn thing, having a *why* to come back to can be just the thing that keeps the team going.

When we work with clients on their change vision, we ask them three questions:

1. In what specific ways will performance be improved at the end of this process?

2. What team behaviors are you looking to see increased and sustained?

3. Why is this performance improvement effort critical?

We recommend that to build a vision statement, the team first brainstorm the answers to each of these questions. The team should then discuss and distill the answers until the key priorities of each question are identified. This doesn't mean that items not chosen at this time won't be addressed at a later point, but the vision must outline performance improvement that is a stretch for the team, but still achievable. If the vision lists twelve specific areas for improvement to achieve in twenty-four months, its resources will be stretched so thin that none of the improvements will get the attention they deserve.

Once the priorities are identified, a subcommittee of two or three people should work together to create a first draft of the vision statement and present it to the whole coalition. If the direction is right, wordsmith the statement until the coalition is satisfied with it. If the direction is lacking, try again. This is a messy process, and it requires far more time than people think it will. It's important to establish a clear destination and a reason for getting there, but don't let perfection keep you from moving forward. This is a situation where complete consensus can actually derail a process. Although consensus is possible, once a majority of the group identifies strongly with a majority of the statement, go ahead and adopt it as a pilot statement. Set a time in the future, say three to four weeks ahead, when the team can come back and edit the statement based on their experience working to achieve the change vision.

Many of our clients find the vision statement step daunting. While the sense of urgency is firmly established and the guiding coalition is on board, actually describing what the end goals look like can seem overwhelming. This happens for many reasons; here are some of the main ones:

- All of your team members have their own, very specific perspective on what needs to change. These perspectives can differ significantly, and opening up dialogue about them can seem scary.

- In today's extremely interconnected, digitally focused world, a change in one system often means changes in many other systems. Considering the impacts of taking just the first step toward higher performance can seem daunting if it means changing the norm.

- Creating a change vision means that the leaders who have established the status quo need to acknowledge that the processes they have been leading aren't working any longer. This can feel like a personal failure. For this reason in particular, it's important to pay due respect to those who have worked hard on behalf of the team and who will now help take the team to a new level of performance.

We once consulted with a financial services firm to develop a change vision for the firm. Change had been needed for so long that the list of desired performance improvements started to seem longer than *War and Peace*. A change vision must be concise to be powerful. It must set challenging expectations, but still be based in reality.

Through in-depth discussion, the financial services firm's guiding coalition recognized that in the first year of the change process, designing a system for individual performance standards, review, and coaching was the most critical change needed to set the stage for long-term growth. Their change vision read as follows: "The Management Team's Vision for Change includes creating a performance management and development system that allows each team member to flourish, foster an environment of continuous improvement, and foster an environment of accountability."

Working with your team to complete a change vision can feel like a challenging undertaking, made even more challenging by the fact that there is no verifiable right or wrong for your particular situation. It's important to keep in mind, if you feel yourself hesitating to undertake the task, that change is even harder when individuals don't understand what they are working so hard for. If your team can't trust that the future will be better than today, then why put in the extra effort, time, and energy to rework processes and *rewire their brains*?

A well-drafted change vision can sustain motivation through difficult times by clearly and concisely reminding team members what they are working together to achieve.

Checklist for Creating a Change Vision

- Schedule at least two meetings dedicated to developing the change vision.

- Brainstorm the answers to the three change vision questions.

- Ensure that the completed vision is specific enough to create alignment and is purposeful enough to communicate why it's so important.

Chapter 2

Getting Stuck

At some point in this process of performance improvement, you will want to run screaming down the hallway. Accept it. This process will not, we repeat *will not*, resemble the motivational posters hanging in your break room. For the sanity of everyone involved, do not hold the expectation that your team will move through this process like a tanned and synchronized crew team effortlessly gliding down a river in a perfect representation of teamwork.

If you prepare the process in the ways we have prescribed and ensure that you are taking into account each piece of the model we lay out for you, you are creating the best possible circumstances for performance improvement to and the changes associated with it to take hold. But achieving your change vision will not be easy. Implementing the changes needed to once again enjoy robust growth will be frustrating, tiring, emotional, and, in our experience, often include some tears.

The process will require a new level of learning, self-awareness, and discipline from everyone on the team. The team must be prepared to move through the most difficult topics and obstacles together. And the team must be prepared to identify when it gets stuck and how to come up with a plan for getting unstuck. In our experience, getting stuck is a result of one of the following:

- A team has failed to identify and implement a critical behavior or system needed for the performance improvement.

- The team has not given enough attention to the brain's need to let go of long-established habits and overcome the emotional attachment to them.

- The change effort is moving faster than is realistic for adoption and learning.

- A topic is so taboo that it has gone without discussion for years and is now a major obstacle on the road to success.

- The system the team is part of is rejecting the change in order to protect its own status quo and is throwing up resistance at every turn.

Often, getting stuck results from a nail-biting-inducing, custom combination of these root causes unique to your situation.

The root causes of getting stuck can seem overwhelming at first. If your team gets stuck, how will you know which root cause or combination of causes is the culprit? Luckily, you don't have to be able to diagnose the cause or causes yourself; you only have to be able to facilitate the discussion with your team.

It's important to pause here and accept a simple fact: You are one of the root causes. If you are the founder or an executive of the organization you seek to grow, there is no escaping the fact that some of your behaviors are contributing to the results you are currently seeing. This book was written for you so that you can up your game while helping your team up theirs. The faster you own and improve your contribution as a leader, the faster you will resume the growth you seek.

Unfreeze, Change, Refreeze

We begin every improvement process with our clients by describing one simple change model: Unfreeze, Change, Refreeze. Kurt Lewin developed this model for change over fifty years ago, and it has inspired decades of scholarly discussion around change leadership. Lucky for us, it endures because of its incredible simplicity. Even the most frustrated team leader, on the verge of throwing in the towel, can use this model to lead powerful discussions around whether or not a team is stuck in its change efforts.

Unfreeze

Now that you understand why the brain holds onto habits so strongly, you can see the need for the first phase of Lewin's model. A team must align around a reason to change and begin to question its own status quo as the foundation for the acceptance and advocacy of any changes in systems and behaviors.

This portion of the process can be the most emotional and can evoke the most resistance. Unfreezing means that all individuals must take a hard look in the mirror at their habits, assumptions, and goals. They have to then question whether these habits, assumptions, and goals still serve them and the organization in the long term. People's reactions to this phase will be determined by how strong their neural links to their habits are and by whether their previous experience with change was positive or negative.

When working to unfreeze, it helps to create a prioritized list of opportunities for performance improvement. Where are the biggest gaps in performance? Where are the biggest risks to long-term success? By identifying these risks, then prioritizing them, you can often build buy-in for the need to change systems, processes, or even organizational structures.

Unfreezing does not occur for everyone at the same time. Often, change leaders will be the first to unfreeze, and they will want to drive like a freight train straight to change. Letting them drive that train would be a mistake. The entire team must work together to ensure that everyone is unfrozen before embarking on change. If individuals are forced into change too quickly, their emotional response will be utter resistance, which will eventually drive the entire team back to the unfreeze stage.

Honor this difficult phase with patience, support, and enough discussion to ensure that the team moves forward together.

A team is unfrozen when they genuinely align around the specific changes that need to be discussed, implemented, and sustained.

Change

The change portion of the Lewin model can be exhilarating. Once the team has identified specific change needs, the possibilities are endless. Clients in this phase have often told us that they haven't felt so engaged in years. One executive said, "I haven't felt so excited about the possibilities of this company since I first joined."

With reinvention, the possible improvements are within reach, the old constraints are gone, and what lies ahead is the promise of a stronger, more effective, and more efficient team. The change phase is where the team moves from recognizing that change is necessary to actually creating a change plan that charts new ways of doing things, in terms of both behaviors and processes.

In the change phase, it's important to keep the engagement and motivation going. Sometimes the discussion around what actually needs to change can become frustrating due to differing perspectives and strong opinions. Also, if an individual is currently benefiting from the way things have been done in the past, that person is going to struggle with letting go of that status quo. Make sure you are aware of these situations ahead of time, and address them appropriately. At these moments, it's handy to refer back to the team's sense of urgency and shared change vision to keep up morale and move through the tough discussions toward resolution and a change plan.

Case Study: Identifying Change

One firm we worked with recognized that they had failed to define a competitive advantage, which meant that they were often losing bids to other service providers who were offering more specific benefits to potential clients. Year-over-year revenue growth was one of the major improvements the organization was striving for.

This firm had a highly innovative and unique pricing structure that was disruptive for the industry and highly beneficial to clients. Unfortunately, employees weren't leveraging this value in marketing or business development opportunities. Ninety-nine percent of this firm's clients were using the innovative pricing structure, but no one in the firm was leveraging it as a marketing differentiator!

In the change phase, the team recognized the need to educate and train employees on the pricing structure. The employees would then need to support the competitive advantage through specific business development behaviors and engagement processes. The pricing structure resulted in profitability only if the employees managed the projects in certain ways, meaning critical processes needed to be refined and implemented. We worked with the team to outline the competitive advantage and critical behaviors and processes, readying them for the refreezing phase.

Refreeze

Any change that is designed and implemented must next become institutionalized within the team or organization. This means that any change implemented needs to become a new standard to which individuals are held accountable. If the performance improvement behavior or system does not become a part of the culture, it will be rejected as a threatening foreign body, leaving the team right back where it began.

Refreezing can take many forms, including a formally adopted policy or process, a trained behavior, a performance management expectation, or even an official metric that is monitored and regularly reported.

You will know that the refreeze stage has begun when change has been implemented and the majority of stakeholders have adopted the performance improvement. There may still be some resisters, but we have found that over time resisters eventually buy in, move to another organization, or need to be let go.

We see many leaders falter when it comes to the refreeze stage. Why? Because ensuring that new systems and behaviors are fully implemented and adopted requires a leader's most valuable resource: time. Leaders must be prepared to spend the time necessary to make institutionalizing the desired systems and behaviors a priority. This requires a high level of discipline and team interaction to overcome latent resistance and avoid falling back into the old status quo.

All too often, leaders receive positive feedback from team members and are lulled into believing that the new behavior or system is as good as implemented. This is rarely the case. The leader must diligently follow through to ensure that adoption is actually occurring.

Think back to the brain biology we discussed earlier. The refreezing portion of the model is where the basal ganglia build new neural links for new habits. Without these new neural links, individuals will not become comfortable with new processes, nor will they be as effective or efficient. Refreezing formalizes a change into a team best practice, creating continued and sustained performance improvement.

Is Lewin's Model Outdated?

Over the past few years, we have come across a number of articles and webinars that declare change leadership a dead skill and Lewin's model outdated. The reasoning behind these declarations is that the ever-increasing pace of change and the level of marketplace turbulence require greater agility than the Lewin model can allow for.

As performance consultants working across many different industries, from tech to engineering, we absolutely agree that the forces that shape organizational performance are now in constant and continuous flux. This flux absolutely does require greater agility from teams, essentially requiring that individuals work together to become a *learning team.*

The problem with treating Lewin's model as a thing of the past is the new expectation that takes its place. We've seen time and again what happens when a leader bypasses any one of the prescribed steps for performance improvement: massive resistance or eventual failure with a cataclysmic loss of trust and morale. Lewin's model works so well because it takes into account the biology of the brain. Yes, it takes time to question our comfortable habits, identify new ones, and implement them sustainably, but ultimately, the time invested in moving through the steps thoughtfully and deliberately saves time down the road.

When Shortcuts Prevent Success

Prior to working with us, one of our clients, a payroll-outsourcing firm, had created a hiring system designed to prevent any major salary and title inconsistencies that might occur as a result of different hiring managers and a rapid hiring timeframe. The system was created because a high number of inconsistencies that occurred during a period of intense company growth were causing a loss of job satisfaction among those employees who realized that some of their team members with similar titles were making far more than they were because of who had hired them.

The firm's team created a checks-and-balances system in which new-hire salaries and titles were checked for consistency and approved before an offer letter was sent to the candidate. Managers throughout the organization agreed that this new system was needed and felt it would be very beneficial. The system was rolled out and... no one adopted it. The team had moved through the first two stages, unfreeze and change, but had incorrectly assumed that a high level of buy-in equaled adoption.

The team had provided no disciplined follow-through, no measurement of success, and no system of accountability to ensure the new system was used or that it worked. The refreeze step was ignored, and the entire effort of the team was wasted on a process that never got off the ground. Needless to say, their morale was higher before they started the change process than after it.

Each and every team performance improvement initiative we support as consultants includes all three phases. Some clients express concern that the process will take too much time. We always ask them how much time they have spent bypassing the process and developing change initiatives that didn't stick. When we look back with them at the months spent on improvements that weren't adopted, they realize that those failed improvements come at a radically higher cost than taking the time to do it right.

In today's world of *right now*, Lewin's model requires time. At first glance, that may seem to put it at a disadvantage. We argue, however, that the team that fails to take into account the brain's biology is at a disadvantage. We are only as agile as our brains. The good news is that with dedicated practice and the disciplined use of Lewin's model, a team becomes more skilled at change and increasingly agile. The more an individual practices adaptability, the faster change occurs. The highest-performing teams don't reject Lewin's model; they become exceptionally efficient at it.

Case Study: Getting Stuck

A medium-sized residential construction firm that had been in business for over thirty years serving the San Francisco Bay Area hired us to assess current performance and identify ways to drive increases in revenue and profitability. The company's experience, reputation, and leadership had pulled it through the financial crisis, but not without scars. Around 2012 the executive team began to recognize the signs of a seriously demoralized workforce, a lack of strategic alignment, and shrinking project profits. Right around the six-month mark of our work, we began to notice symptoms that the team was stuck. They were still very engaged in the process during our consulting sessions, professing how much they felt themselves changing during the process. Yet the particular systems and processes we had designed together were not being fully implemented and were starting to stack up on a to-do list.

The CFO anxiously described the situation over the phone: "I feel like momentum has just slowed to nothing. Everyone wants this to happen, but we just aren't following up." Her anxiety was warranted; after all, without those systems and processes, any positive changes the team experienced would be short lived and unsustainable.

We held an in-depth check-in meeting with the team to identify the root cause of the halted progress. On a whiteboard we created three columns with these headings: Unfreeze, Change, and Refreeze.

We asked the seven team members to put a mark under the phase of the model that represented their perception of the team's current state. One outlier marked to the left of Unfreeze, and one marked to the far right of Change, but the remaining five team members clustered their marks right at the end of Unfreeze.

We led a discussion around what these results meant to the team, and the members came to the agreement that while they were unfreezing, change wasn't occurring. With this level of buy-in, it was time to identify the root cause. In describing this case to others, we have heard time and again, "Oh, I've seen that. Clearly they didn't have enough buy-in from the start, that's an easy one."

That assumption, like many assumptions, is completely false. The team had poured their hearts into the process in a way that we wish all clients would. They were genuinely engaged, participatory, and thrilled about the possibility of improvement.

We used *why* questions—without judgment—to identify the causes behind the mounting list of past-due implementation deadlines. At first the feeling in the room was uncomfortable. After all, we were laying bare a list of things the team had committed to do but had not yet accomplished. We gently pushed on, with curiosity and interest, and finally one project manager quietly said, "Honestly, I have so many other things to do, I just never make the time to discuss my action items with the team. I tend to focus on the items that are driving revenue, and these just never seem to make it to the top of the list." The others nodded in agreement and understanding.

Another project manager then offered, "You know, besides these meetings, we never get together just as a team to make sure these items are getting done."

In this case, the team's major obstacle was not having a system of accountability in place that would allow for questions to be asked, commitments to be kept, and time needed for follow through to be protected. The lack of progress in this case was also tightly linked to the root cause of the CEO's apathy towards consistent accountability. Because he hadn't changed his behavior, his team hadn't changed theirs and the company was not achieving an acceptable return on investment for the team's work, the millions of dollars in equipment or even our consulting engagement.

The team agreed to meet weekly for thirty minutes to check in on implementation progress. With this new plan in place, individuals had the sense that working on their action items was a greater priority, and they also felt supported by the team if they ran into an unforeseen issue.

As a team leader, it's important to stop your team or yourself from going on autopilot when it comes to driving change and performance improvement. Remember, because of how our brains store habits, autopilot most likely means going back to what felt comfortable before the change process started. Even the most motivated teams sometimes find themselves slowly backsliding toward the old ways of working, especially in times of stress. During this phase, keep a lookout for old habits, processes, and systems creeping back into daily operations. If you see this happening, schedule a team conversation and identify how best to ensure that progress continues.

Chapter 3

Accountability

A growing financial services firm engaged us to support their performance improvement initiative. Their objectives included increasing team and individual effectiveness for very specific revenue growth and profitability targets. The firm was full of brilliant leaders with bright ideas and energy to spare. In fact, when they engaged us, they shared with us the work they had already done toward performance improvement, which was far more than the typical client does. Yet for some reason, the previous performance improvement effort had never seemed to take hold. And despite the high competency among the leadership team, turnover in the firm remained stubbornly high.

The "aha" moment came during a meeting early in the engagement with the leadership team. Together we had already identified small, specific action items to be implemented immediately. These action items would affect the staff and require their support. We then identified the implementation plan and began wrapping up the meeting. One of the managers, who had been looking concerned and pensive for the last quarter of an hour, lifted his head and gravely asked, "What do we do when staff tells us they don't want to?" Others in the group nodded in agreement, looking relieved that someone had asked the question weighing heavily on their minds.

I inquired, "Does this happen often?"

"Often enough," the manager said.

"How do you normally handle that situation?" I asked.

"Whatever we have requested often just doesn't get done. It gets dropped and not picked back up. We aren't very good at that conversation, which means staff is pretty comfortable saying, 'I don't want to.'"

It was as if a lightning bolt had been sent straight from the sky into that conference room—suddenly, it was blindingly apparent why this organization was struggling despite all the positive characteristics it had going for it.

This brilliant team lacked accountability on an individual, team, and systemic level, meaning that no matter what innovative initiative leadership designed, it was doomed to fail during implementation.

An Epidemic

When we began consulting, we took for granted that when solutions were uncovered and action items listed, those action items would actually lead to, well... action. We were fascinated (okay, stunned) to find that the common thread running through all of our clients was a colossal lack of accountability. Of course, it makes sense. Without accountability, any proposed improvements don't receive the necessary support and discipline to ensure that they are actually implemented. The status quo remains a force with powerful momentum, and an action item without accountability can't stand up to it.

Time and again, firms told us stories of previous attempts at improvement that were thwarted as soon as it came time for team behaviors to actually change. If change resisters experience no consequences for failing to implement or follow up, they learn to resist early and often. This habit overwhelms any improvement initiative and traps the team and organization in a safe and comfortable status quo. With this no-consequences system in place, employees see little reason to expend the effort to change. How motivated would you be to change or take action when you know there is little upside and almost no chance of long-term success?

Stanford professors Jeffrey Pfeffer and Robert Sutton had the same stunning accountability revelation, watching as class after class of the future leaders they taught failed again and again to practice with their teams what they learned at Stanford. Pfeffer and Sutton coauthored a book on the subject called *The Knowing-Doing Gap.*

Pfeffer and Sutton recognized the lack-of-accountability epidemic across organizations of all types and sizes: "There are a number of studies within single industries demonstrating that there are superior ways of managing people and organizing their work. Yet, although these superior management practices are reasonably well-known, diffusion proceeds slowly and fitfully, and backsliding is common."[7]

We often refer to this as *the accountability epidemic*, because for some reason, we have found a pervasive lack of strong and consistent accountability in nearly every client team we've worked with. If we go back to biology, and consider that collaboration is one of the attributes credited with the evolution and survival of our species throughout time, it makes sense that we tend to strive for collaborative, positive relationships. Many managers harbor deep fears that instituting accountability could ruin a trusting, positive, collaborative relationship with a direct report. We assure you that accountability, when done right, can actually strengthen such relationships while also leading to marked increases in performance. We'll outline exactly what that looks like in the next section.

Accountability, a Definition

Before diving into the root causes of the lack-of-accountability epidemic, it's important to clearly define exactly what we mean by *accountability*. Part of the problem with accountability is that individuals often each have their own personal definition of it. They picked it up in childhood or adolescence and never discussed with their manager or coworker what it means for their adult team.

If you do a web search for the term *accountability*, you will come up with over 54 *million* websites and this web dictionary definition: "The fact or condition of being accountable." Essentially, the most unhelpful definition *ever*.

In our effort to nail down the elusive meaning of this word, we engaged the opinions of many of our executive clients. Some felt strongly that accountability is entirely up to the individual, in that it is the responsibility of the individual alone to keep any commitments made.

Other executives saw accountability as a managerial responsibility, meaning the leadership of an organization has a duty to hold individuals responsible to the commitments they have made.

After exhaustive research and studying highly successful, accountable teams, we have come to realize accountability is both an individual function and a leadership function, with one more crucial ingredient: a system.

While it's not as concise as the one-line web dictionary definition, we have leveraged this definition of accountability to increase team performance:

> *Accountability is the assumption of responsibility and consequences for actions, decisions, and policies. A level of ownership that includes making, keeping, and answering for personal commitments.*

> *Accountability includes a system of feedback, tracking, and support to ensure commitments are kept and results are reached. It encompasses the obligation to report, explain, and be answerable for consequences. Accountability is a way of working and living, not just a consequence for poor performance.*

An individual or team models accountability when they demonstrate the ownership necessary for achieving the desired business results and understand how their actions affect others.

When a team seeks to instill a culture of accountability, they work together to increase the accountability of the individuals for the benefit of the whole. When both leadership and the team are comfortable holding individuals to their commitments, individuals take even greater personal responsibility. They become more aware of the impact they have on the team's performance and are willing to do what it takes to ensure their commitments are kept.

An Engine of Continued Success

This powerful cycle of increased individual responsibility and team performance leads to great agility and continuous improvement. A company like Toyota, famous for its continuous improvement culture, reaps incredible efficiencies because factory-floor workers are quick to share new ideas and opportunities for process improvement, resulting in what's often referred to today as a *lean*, or efficient and effective operation.

Fine, Hansen, and Roggenhofer's "From Lean to Lasting: Making Operational Improvements Stick," published in *McKinsey* in 2008, discusses the incredible complexity and challenge associated with creating a culture that continually reinforces the performance improvement changes an organization imple-ments. "Recently, organizations as diverse as steelmakers, insurance companies, and public sector agencies have benefited from 'leaning' their operations with Toyota's now-classic approach: eliminating waste, variability, and inflexibility... The broader challenge underlying such problems is integrating the better known 'hard' operational tools and approaches—such as just-in-time production—with the 'soft' side, including the development of leaders who can help teams continuously identify and make efficiency improvements, link and align the boardroom with the shop floor, and build the technical and interpersonal skills that make efficiency benefits real."[8]

By taking the time to ensure you have established a solid change foundation for your team, then approaching the performance improvement with patience and discipline, you *can* create a culture of accountability—a culture that ensures the changes needed in your team can be sustained far into the future.

Obstacles

Four main obstacles stand in the way of teams creating a culture of accountability and reaching the performance improvement within their grasp: a lack of patience, the tyranny of the now, a fear of holding individuals to their commitments, and strong cultural norms. Does one of these sound familiar? Oh, all four of them do. Yep, we hear that all the time. Don't worry, we're going to break down each one so you are prepared to be the management rock star you've always know you could be, leading your team over, around, and straight through accountability obstacles.

A Lack of Patience

Here's some depressing news: Gallup reports that over 70 percent of change initiatives fail. What else does Gallup say? "They don't have to."[9] We couldn't agree more. Many change initiatives never go through the steps we have already taken you through, which means they begin on extremely shaky foundations. So many teams embark on performance improvement initiatives that have unrealistic expectations in terms of both time and results.

You now know the neuroscience, and you understand why it takes serious time, commitment, and discipline to break down old habits and build new ones. Many team leaders and CEOs we've worked with have been tempted to give up the change effort after a few months because they weren't seeing the results they had secretly expected.

This frustration from the leader can become contagious and drain morale. A team leader or CEO has the benefit of being the person driving the change; *of course* they are going to adapt more quickly. It's a leader's patience for allowing others to test new behaviors and for coaching and building morale when things get stuck that can truly make the difference between failure and success. Remember, accountability is more than just making sure people do what they say. Sometimes accountability means helping them through the obstacle that's preventing them from acting—and that can mean coaching them through a change in behavior over time.

The Tyranny of the Now

An organization can't stop operations just because it's undergoing a performance improvement initiative. This means that day-to-day priorities will continue to demand the time of those who most need time to plan, implement, and lead change.

In many performance improvement initiatives, a team or organization's current results are heading downhill fast. This means that the team may be trying to plot an entirely new course while simultaneously trying to bail water out of a sinking ship. Talk about a stressful environment.

In this type of environment, daily fires need extinguishing, and a team often feels they are playing whack-a-mole rather than making true progress. When the daily fires seem to require 100 percent of everyone's time, the excuses for not seeing change initiatives through are abundant. Accountability and the performance improvement effort suffer greatly if a team is unwilling to make the change effort just as important as daily operations. The tyranny of the now will overwhelm the change effort, creating a slow downward spiral of lost accountability and progress. Teams experiencing this lack of accountability often look back after six months and wonder, "We've been so busy, why aren't things getting better?"

A team that refuses to let the tyranny of the now dominate their time may experience additional conflict as they work to improve behaviors and systems. It's critical to know that this is temporary, and as the behaviors and systems are implemented, adopted, and held accountable, the daily fires become fewer and fewer.

A Fear of Holding Individuals to Their Commitments

There are a myriad of reasons that leaders may be uncomfortable holding their direct reports and team members to commitments. Perhaps a team member is a brilliantly technical individual who was promoted for technical skill but was never trained in motivating or managing others. Or perhaps this member's upbringing promoted a "keep quiet and don't make waves" approach to relationships.

No matter what the underlying cause, an individual leading a change effort needs to be extremely comfortable with holding others to their commitments in supportive, inquisitive ways. We'll explore exactly how to do that shortly.

We have often encountered team members apologizing for their leadership's lack of accountability by telling us, "He is just really uncomfortable with confrontation; I can understand why he doesn't like bringing up unfinished tasks." The idea that accountability equals confrontation is dangerous, yet all too common. If you or others on your team classify holding others to their commitments or discussing sensitive topics as confrontation, it's possible that the team won't achieve its true potential.

Strong Cultural Norms

If an organization has spent years in a steady, stable status quo, odds are its team members are extremely comfortable. As we've discussed earlier, this is why fostering a strong sense of urgency and understanding of the brain's biology is critical prior to embarking on a performance improvement initiative.

Very often, if an organization has maintained the status quo for some time, team members have not engaged in questioning and reflection about their performance or behaviors. When a team member has to shift from an abundance of autonomy and comfort to increased collaboration, challenge, and accountability, the pesky basal ganglia can kick in and foment resistance. The previous, strong cultural norms of performance acceptance will absolutely fight to keep control. Pfeffer and Sutton elaborate on this phenomenon in *The Knowing-Doing Gap*:

Precedent, when inappropriately applied, can interfere with both the process of learning and of applying knowledge to enhance organizational performance. Perhaps the most serious problem with precedent is that it is used automatically, almost without thought. Scholars who study this kind of thinking and the actions associated with it have described it using terms such as "habits of mind," and "performance programs." Ellen Langer, a psychologist who has done the most work in this area, described mindlessness as situations in which people act without paying attention to what they are doing. "The individual becomes mindlessly trapped by categories that were previously created when the person was in a mindful mode." When people in an organization engage in mindless acts based on precedent, such behavior precludes them from even considering whether practices need to be reexamined.[10]

When the resistance borne of past precedents and cultural norms rears its head, leaders often fear that insisting on accountability will cause team members to leave the team. Consequently, the leaders back off working to ensure that change-effort commitments are kept.

It's true that turnover may happen—after all, you are leading your team members to a new, higher-performing version of the team. Sometimes a few team members are threatened by the change or simply aren't on board. The question becomes, is it more crucial to maintain the stable status quo with the team exactly as is, or reach a new level of performance with those who are willing to make the effort?

Crucial Accountability

By taking the time and developing the discipline to prepare your team for a performance improvement effort, as outlined in the past two chapters, you are greatly increasing the chances that your effort will succeed. The team will have a strong foundation upon which to build momentum.

Momentum gets you going; accountability keeps you going. Accountability ensures that commitments are kept and change continues to improve performance. As such, it can be the difference between completing a successful performance initiative and ending up as a disappointing Gallup statistic.

Necessary for what Lewin calls refreezing, accountability ensures that the new behaviors and systems you need to succeed will stay in place for the long term. Any one of the four obstacles to accountability can derail your change effort to the point of failure. Don't take them lightly, and don't accept them as team habit.

Returning to our definition of accountability, putting in place the following key elements will ensure that your team is prepared to incorporate accountability into their culture:

1. Clear understanding and individual ownership of commitments and consequences

2. A disciplined system of check-ins and reporting

3. The team and individual ability to hold others responsible for their actions and coach them to success

Teams often have one or two of these elements already built in, but one element is almost always missing. Take a moment to consider which elements are present with your current team: Do you decide on action, but without having an individual own a particular task or result? Are you disappointed when, after building a shared change vision and identifying action items, everything is exactly the same three months later? Do deadlines pass with no acknowledgement or deeper discussion of why they were missed? Do individuals on your team accept subpar performance because they don't want to rock the boat or aren't comfortable with confrontation? Each of these scenarios can be a symptom of a lack of accountability on your team that will at worst derail the performance improvement process and at best slow it to a frustrating crawl.

Making Accountability a Habit is as Easy as 1, 2, 3

Believe it or not, increasing accountability doesn't take as much effort and time as you might think. A few fairly simple tactics can make a huge difference and lead to a culture of accountability. Approach each of the three tactics discussed below with discipline and patience, knowing you have to get past that habit gatekeeper, the basal ganglia.

Tactic 1: A clear understanding and individual ownership of commitments and consequences

- When designing goals and processes, be as specific as possible to ensure clarity. When in doubt, ask a team member to reflect the commitment back to you to ensure clarity.

- Make sure every action item has an owner responsible for managing its implementation and reporting on its result. Others may play supporting roles, but one person and one person alone should own the item itself.

- Ask team members up front what they foresee as potential threats to the action item. Take a proactive approach and address the threats before they derail the plan.

- While the owner of an action item should have most of the say in *how* results are obtained, the team becomes even more engaged and supportive when given the opportunity to offer thoughts and ideas up front.

Tactic 2: A disciplined system of check-ins and reporting

- The system of check-ins and reporting can take several different forms depending on the team and the organization; we will discuss these forms in greater depth later. We recommend one-on-one meetings between leaders and their direct reports monthly, as well as a team check-in with time for discussion either weekly or biweekly.

- Individuals assigned ownership of action items need to prepare a status update that documents successes or obstacles to share and discuss with the group.

- Leadership needs to remember that a meeting is a waste of time if check-ins become stale, boring, and lacking in meaningful dialogue. Interest will wane and attendance will soon follow suit. Suddenly, dentist appointments and client conference calls will always seem to get scheduled during check-in time. Keep tying efforts and discussion back to the shared vision and sense of urgency. Use lots of questions to engage participants and keep the meetings meaningful.

Tactic 3: The establishment of the team's and individuals' responsibility to hold each other responsible for their actions and coach each other to success

- When an action item's deadline has passed, it's entirely appropriate to ask "What were the biggest obstacles to completing this action?" Very often, the answer will be that fires needed extinguishing or there just wasn't enough time. As we mentioned before, not committing sufficient time to the change effort is one of its major derailers. If time is the issue, ask team members what they need in terms of support to ensure they can complete the action item by a new, agreed-upon deadline.

- Sometimes, between the time individuals take ownership of an action item and the completion date, their basal ganglia kick in and say "Hey! This isn't how we do things! You were perfectly comfortable before, why mess with it?" This can lead to the scientific diagnosis of "foot dragging" and the person reporting to the team, "I'm not sure this task actually needs to be done; here's why..." Leaders need to hear them out. They may have sound logic, and the task they took ownership of may not actually *be* the best next step. Before you accept this, however, return to the shared vision of change and the reasons for your team's sense of urgency to gauge whether this task really isn't necessary or if it does, in fact, support the desired performance improvement.

- Leaders need to be prepared to coach. Performance improvement is difficult work for even the highest performers. You can't expect a major league baseball team to make it to the World Series without strong coaching; likewise, you can't expect your team to establish entirely new behaviors and systems without strong coaching. Your team will need positive feedback on their efforts, and they need constructive feedback when their performance isn't getting them where they want to be. Your feedback should be more positive than constructive—this puts both the team and the leader at ease and builds the solid foundation of trust needed when the conversations turn tough.

Accountability is the fuel for change. With our biological bent toward a comfortable status quo, resistance to a new way of doing things is strong on any team. Accountability ensures a continual progression forward. Without accountability, any performance improvement effort will sputter and eventually die out.

Today's rapidly changing marketplace demands continuous improvement. This book will give you the tools you need to continually identify opportunities for higher team performance and execute accordingly. Every tool also plays a part in building the strong accountability infrastructure you need to ensure that your team stays efficient, effective, agile, and *continuously* improving.

Part II

Laying The Foundation

Chapter 4

Purpose

Take a moment to consider the images your brain conjures when you read the term *organizational purpose*. If you are like most of our clients, it conjures up either some sort of generic motivational statement hanging in the lobby or a slightly uncomfortable feeling that we've veered off the course of turning a profit and into something entirely too psycho-babbly or touchy-feely. (Yes, real feedback from clients.)

What if we told you that *purpose* is neither meaningless decoration nor pop-psychology jargon, but rather a concept that can actually transform your team's financial performance? Suddenly, purpose becomes a lot more interesting.

Purpose isn't the only key to setting up your team for success. In the next two chapters, we will continue to explore how to build the foundation for your team's performance improvement by determining your values and competitive advantage.

When combined, these three frameworks—purpose, values, and competitive advantage—make up your team's very own best practices manual. Imagine each of your team members embarking on each new day knowing exactly which behaviors will drive success year after year.

Some may roll their eyes at the idea of values and purpose as the starting point of financial success. Frankly, before working with so many teams on performance improvement, we would have rolled our eyes, too. Before we conducted our research and worked as consultants, we thought values and purpose were website fodder that no one actually paid attention to.

We were very wrong. Research shows that companies that identify their purpose and values, then stand behind them day in and day out, end up with much fatter bottom lines and much happier shareholders than companies that think of purpose and values just as cultural fluff and stuff.

Outperforming the Competition

How much of a financial impact are we talking about? More than you think. In 2007, *Firms of Endearment* reported on twenty-eight corporations that the authors had rigorously researched and identified as truly loved by all of their stakeholders. The companies include Amazon, Trader Joe's, and REI. Each of these companies has an overarching purpose that aligns the interests of the various stakeholders, including employees, clients, and shareholders. It's important to note that none of these companies makes increasing shareholder value its priority purpose.

The authors wanted to write about how these companies sustained greatness in the eyes of their employees, clients, and shareholders. When they analyzed the stock returns of the publicly traded "firms of endearment" against the S&P 500 between the years 1996 and 2006, they were shocked to discover that the firms returned an astonishing 1,026 percent—almost eight times more than the S&P 500's 122 percent for the same time period.[11] So, what do the authors hypothesize as the reason for such incredible financial returns? According to the authors, the firms "engender such loyalty and a sense of common cause with their stakeholders that they seem far better able to withstand downturns than their competitors."[12]

A 2005 British study by The Work Foundation bolsters the findings of *Firms of Endearment*. The study analyzed the performance of more than three thousand firms in order to identify the distinctions between the best and worst performers. This study found that "in terms of added value, the top third of firms out-perform the bottom two-thirds by £1,600 (approximately $2,672.00) per worker per annum."[13]

Among the characteristics that distinguished the highest-performing firms, the researchers observed open sharing of information among employees, a constant questioning of the status quo for continuous improvement, and, "at the heart of the [Company Performance Index] is the notion of the sustainable high-success company that understands its 'reason to be' and then pursues it wholeheartedly, supported by a set of values that are mutually reinforcing."[14]

Our experience with clients correlates with The Work Foundation findings. A defined "reason to be" combined with a clear set of values and a defined competitive advantage are not marketing extras. Together they form the essential foundation for long-term team success.

In the next few chapters, we will answer all your burning questions, including: How does something as nontechnical as *purpose* translate into dollars? How do we define our values when we can't agree on where to go for lunch? What is the difference between purpose and strategy?

Purpose and Bottom Line

Let's focus now on how purpose affects the bottom line and why defining it is a key step towards increased growth. First, we need to take a moment to define the word *purpose*. When we refer to *purpose*, we are referring to an organizational "reason to be" that has a lasting, positive impact. A performance-driving purpose builds the psychological link between individual employees and something bigger than themselves. This link serves both to align employees toward the same goal and to increase motivation.

Let's look at some hypothetical examples of organizational purpose statements that would *not* result in the type of psychological commitment we are aiming for:

- "We exist to give shareholders the largest return for their investment."

- "Our purpose is to produce more tube socks than any other tube sock company in the market."

- "We work at all costs to grow our revenues by ten percent year over year."

- "Nothing means more to us than dominating the international Greek yogurt market."

Each of these purposes is extrinsic, meaning the outcomes of these efforts are external rewards versus positive social outcomes that lead to internal satisfaction. While this type of goal can be part of an overall plan for performance, it will not result in the deep connection that convinces employees to give their discretionary effort. Organizational purposes that are intrinsic, however, do create the deep psychological bond that increases motivation, psychological well-being, and loyalty to the team.

Here are examples of purpose statements from organizations that enjoy consistent success:

Proctor and Gamble: We will provide branded products and services of superior quality and value that improve the lives of the world's consumers, now and for generations to come. As a result, consumers will reward us with leadership sales, profit and value creation, allowing our people, our shareholders, and the communities in which we live and work to prosper.

Starbucks: To inspire and nurture the human spirit—one person, one cup, and one neighborhood at a time.

Patagonia: Build the best product, cause no unnecessary harm, use business to inspire and implement solutions to the environmental crisis.

What do these purpose statements have in common? A clear "reason to be" that is even more meaningful than profit. Sure these companies produce cleaning products, coffee, and jackets, but they are committed to making a lasting and positive impact on the world through the products they offer.

The crucial combination of purpose, values, and a clear competitive advantage tap into two key team performance concepts: intrinsic motivation—essentially the fire and passion individuals have for their work—and alignment—how cohesively individuals work together to accomplish a shared goal.

Intrinsic Motivation

The reason that a clear purpose drives motivation derives from our most primal psychological needs. The work of Christopher Niemiec, Richard Ryan, and Edward Deci has done wonders to shed light on the connection between intrinsic (internally driven) motivation and organizational purpose. These researchers have identified three basic needs that drive increased psychological health and satisfaction: autonomy, competence, and relatedness.[15]

The third basic need, relatedness, is most relevant to purpose. Creating a common purpose that all employees contribute to makes them feel strongly connected to others in the organization and in the service of something greater than themselves. Niemiec, Ryan, and Deci found that when individuals worked in environments where these three psychological needs were met, correlated outcomes included better psychological health and the development of intrinsic motivation.[16]

The Secret Sauce

Intrinsic motivation is the secret sauce of purpose-driven companies. When employees are intrinsically motivated, they act from their own internal commitment and desire to perform at a high level to deliver greatness, even if it requires the occasional personal sacrifice. Let's look at that another way: If we asked you to describe an ideal employee, wouldn't you say something along the lines of "She would constantly seek to deliver high-quality work, even if it meant going above and beyond her normal job expectations."

An employee who exhibits this type of behavior consistently over time is an employee with strong intrinsic motivation. To cultivate this behavior on your team, you need to create an environment in which autonomy, competence, and relatedness are present.

We have found that focusing first on relatedness sparks the intrinsic motivation, paving the way for increased effort and, in turn, greater autonomy and competence.

The work of Niemiec, Ryan, and Deci also explores the impact of extrinsic, or external, motivators. "In contrast, attainment of the extrinsic aspirations for money, fame, and image was unrelated to basic psychological need satisfaction and related slightly negatively to psychological health."[17] We need to be careful not to oversimplify the relationship between external rewards or incentives and motivation. The relationship is complex and situational. Of course successful businesses are going to pursue profit, and successful nonprofits are going to seek widespread impact. The point these researchers make is that leveraging intrinsic motivation as a primary driver instills commitment by fulfilling psychological needs, something that extrinsic motivators alone cannot achieve. Remember, it's not that extrinsic motivators don't work, it's that they aren't a complete picture, and when applied incorrectly, they can hyper-focus motivation and create unintended behavioral consequences.

Commonly, companies seek to elicit motivation through external rewards and incentives. While this can work in some specific cases, as Daniel Pink laid out so eloquently in his groundbreaking book, *Drive*, the results can turn into a twisted version of expected outcomes and sometimes can even be counterproductive. "In real life our behavior is far more complex than the textbook allows and often confounds the idea that we're purely rational. We don't save enough for retirement even though it's to our clear economic advantage to do so. We hang on to bad investments longer than we should, because we feel sharper pain from losing money than we do from gaining the exact same amount... Indeed the very premise of extrinsic incentives is that we'll always respond rationally to them. But even most economists don't believe that anymore. Sometimes these motivators work. Often they don't."[18]

Pink cites Bruno Frey, a prominent economist at the University of Zurich, who argues that "intrinsic motivation is of *great importance* for all economic activities. It is inconceivable that people are motivated solely or even mainly by external incentives."[19]

The Unintended Consequences of a Great Bonus Plan

One of our most successful clients, an engineering firm, wanted its engineers to increase their focus on billable work. Creating an incentive program that gave the engineers a percentage of the income from billable work curbed their tendency toward perfectionism, which had taken up hours and hours of nonbillable time. The company became more efficient.

As the same company grew, however, the firm's leaders had to rethink the incentive program as the focus on billable hours became too strong, and employees became less likely to take on critical internal projects that would potentially reduce their billable hours. Creating external motivation through incentives and rewards can sharpen focus and change behavior, but this client's focus on external motivation is a good example of how extrinsic incentives can go wrong. The organization lacked an overarching purpose, and in an effort to grow quickly, the leadership had focused strongly on billable hours. This resulted in an unhealthy, unbalanced prioritization of revenue over crucial internal projects. The focus on billable hours even resulted in unethical behavior by some employees to maximize their bonuses.

We definitely recommend further researching balanced reward and compensation plans before you design one for your team, but the core message here is that, as shown in *Firms of Endearment*, absent a deep, intrinsic motivation to contribute to a well-defined, central purpose, your team will lack a solid foundation for alignment. This creates a motivation vacuum, and, in the absence of strong intrinsic motivation, individuals will focus on extrinsic rewards, even to the long-term detriment of the team.

The research clearly shows that to increase company performance overall and develop intrinsic motivation, nothing compares to creating an environment with a clear sense of shared purpose in which autonomy and competence can flourish.

The dream team members who give their all and regularly reach above and beyond do so because they have forged a deep psychological commitment to the purpose of the organization and their job. It's through deep psychological commitment that purpose translates into bottom-line success.

Here are a handful of examples of how purpose can enhance efficiency and profitability through intrinsic motivation:

- Employees with strong psychological commitment deliver much more of that magical attribute, discretionary effort.

- *Firms of Endearment* authors found that the client experience of companies with a clear "reason to be" bred loyalty and positive word of mouth.

- Employees often leave an organization once their psychological commitment is broken. A strong purpose can strengthen that commitment, resulting in higher retention.

- Intrinsically motivated employees will be more invested in solving the problems that prevent growth or goal achievement, paving the way for long-term success.

At first glance these outcomes can seem qualitative or even nebulous. But imagine the performance of a team whose members act only for their own self-interest, that considers clients to be annoyances, and where no one will take on the toughest problems because, frankly, they just don't give a damn.

Compare that image with the image of a team that brings the attributes listed above. Which team will perform better in the marketplace? Our combined research and experience has shown us it's the high-performing team with a clearly defined core purpose.

Alignment

Picture for a moment your entire team getting into a small boat. Once they sit down, they are each told to plan how they can most efficiently reach the destination that means the most to them, but they aren't able to communicate with each other. Then each person is given a paddle and told to do whatever is needed to reach the chosen destination. What happens?

Some individuals will start paddling immediately. Some will try to get the others' attention and signal their thoughts. Others will promptly jump out of the boat and swim for shore, abandoning the team. In other words, the team will be about as productive as a team working together without a common purpose.

Every individual brings to an organization his or her own personal motivations. Storied Harvard professor David McClelland famously outlined three basic but very different motivations that drive individuals to act: achievement, power, and affiliation or relationships. According to McClelland's motivational needs theory, the actions of each team member are driven primarily by one of these three motivators.

It is key to remember that your entire team may have a mix of motivations driving its performance. One employee may be working solely for the compensation to care for his family, another might be driven to seek her next promotion, and another may be angling to have the greatest influence with clients. Each of these different motivations can lead to very positive outcomes, but on a team without a shared purpose, differing motivations can lead to inconsistent team actions and unpredictable results.

An overarching purpose does not replace an individual's primary motivational driver, nor should it. Variations in motivations give us the balance we need for a sustainable, high-performing team. The overarching purpose serves to focus and unite team members' individual motivations around a clear and common outcome.

Distinct from strategic alignment (also known as line of sight, which we will discuss in Chapter 7), shared purpose aligns the deeply held *motivations* of team members, not just their actions and goals. In the best companies in the world, purpose creates alignment within the current workforce and also weeds out applicants who don't truly buy in. Companies such as Google, Whole Foods, and Costco ensure that their greater purpose will be met by hiring those who are strongly driven by the companies' core purposes.

Changing the Game

In "Building a Game-Changing Talent Strategy," Douglas Ready, Linda Hill, and Robert Thomas explain that "game-changers are clear about the purpose for which they exist. They know that performance is the route to remaining competitive. And they are adamant that their principles will see them through good times and bad. A company's talent managers can support its objectives by articulating up front that it demands enthusiastic buy-in to its core purpose. Nonbelievers need not apply."[20]

Beyond increasing the performance of your current team, creating a clear core purpose for your team that drives motivation and success also builds the foundation for a strong employment brand. An employment brand with a strong, articulated purpose attracts high-performing talent who want to be part of a winning team, setting the stage for sustainable high performance.

Returning to the concept of intrinsic motivation: A team will be much more closely aligned when each member is intrinsically motivated to perform. Individuals who believe deeply in what the organization is trying to achieve tend to contribute more discretionary effort than individuals who are motivated primarily by money.

When an organization has a clear purpose, a set of mutually reinforcing values, and a defined competitive advantage, teams have the information they need to commit deeply and perform highly, even with differing individual motivations.

If the same team that climbed into that boat had been given a common purpose with clear guiding principles and a strategy for leveraging their strengths, they wouldn't have floundered in the water, sending individuals overboard in the process. Instead, they would have set their sights forward and worked together to reach their destination as quickly as possible.

In 2013, Deloitte conducted a core beliefs and culture survey to explore how core corporate beliefs and values drive business outcomes. The survey results displayed a clear distinction between organizations with purpose and those without.

Respondents who said their organization had a strong sense of purpose were not only more likely to say their company had performed well financially over the last year (90 percent) and historically (91 percent) but also to say their company had a distinct brand that stood out among competitors (91 percent), strong customer satisfaction (94 percent) and strong employee satisfaction (79 percent).

By comparison, of the respondents who said their organization did not have a strong purpose, far fewer said their company had performed well financially over the last year (65 percent) or historically (66 percent). They were also less likely to say their organization had a distinct brand that stood out among competitors (61 percent), had strong customer satisfaction (63 percent) and strong employee satisfaction (19 percent).[21]

It's important to recognize that this survey doesn't measure whether the companies with a strong sense of purpose definitively perform better financially, have a stronger brand, or greater customer satisfaction. What the survey shows is that employees who perceive a strong purpose for their work *are more likely to say* their organization performs better.

We could spend pages dissecting the various meanings of phrases such as "more likely" in this survey, but at the core of the findings is a statistically significant difference in how employees *perceive* organizational performance when they feel part of an organization with a strong sense of purpose. The perception of these employees might be right on target, and the *Firms of Endearment* study would certainly align with the finding that purpose-driven organizations do, in fact, perform better against competition.

The Link Between Purpose and Employee Satisfaction

Either way, consider how the employee satisfaction numbers track with the other statistics listed in the survey: Seventy-nine percent of employees who perceived a strong sense of purpose in their organizations also reported strong employee satisfaction, compared with just nineteen percent of employees who did not perceive a strong sense of purpose in their organization. Which organizations do you think are going to have to spend more money to hire and attempt to retain high performers? Again, given how expensive high turnover rates can be, supporting employee satisfaction with a strong sense of purpose not only aligns employees with a shared motivation but also in many ways supports bottom-line results.

Defining Purpose

Ready to reap the benefits of a motivated and aligned team, but nervous about the process? Don't worry! It's fun, and it elicits lots of meaningful participation. What continues to amaze us year after year is watching that quiet, slightly disconnected and skeptical employee you find on every team spark to life when the purpose exercise begins.

Remember, being a part of something larger than oneself and relating deeply to others are core psychological needs. When you tap into those needs through the purpose exercise, you will be shocked by the degree to which individuals attach deep meaning to their work. Are there individuals who truly just show up for a paycheck? Yes, but they definitely aren't the majority of your team. Most if not all the individuals on your team are there because they believe in something. You need to find out what that something is.

As with most of the work in this book, you'll notice some hesitation and tension at first. When you feel it, own it. Know that only the highest performing teams in the world spend time on this work because it's challenging. It's much easier to show up every day, produce some work, and send out a week's worth of direct deposits. But you know your team will never get better and reach their full potential that way. Choose the path of some resistance and watch as the challenge shapes and molds your team into something much stronger.

When you start this exercise, go in with an open mind. Your idea of team purpose may not be the same as the rest of the group's. The more open you are, the closer you will get to the true, driving "reason to be."

Take Action: Defining Purpose

The team

The team chosen should include all founders, the team or organization leader, and a representative of the organization's guiding coalition, with a maximum of seven people. Representatives of different functions and levels of management are needed for diversity of perspective and organizational buy-in later.

Hardware needed

- At least one easel with a giant notepad, preferably with adhesive on the back
- Markers for brainstorming on the notepad

Exercise outline

First session

Before you begin the purpose exercise, make sure you have completed the three steps for setting up a successful change listed in Part I. For the first hour of this session, gather the team and share with them the research we have shared with you. During this hour, it's important to give some examples of purpose statements and discuss what purpose is and what it isn't.

During the second hour, ask your team two questions:

1. In what ways does our team have a positive impact on the world?

2. If money were not a concern, describe why you might volunteer to do your job. What positive impact would drive you to offer your time this way?

Take notes on every single answer on the notepad. Feel free to post them up around the room. Next, ask the team members to jot down these questions and reflect on them over the next week to see what emerges.

Second session

Ask team members to add any new thoughts to the notes you took during the first session. Now, work together to eliminate any statements of purpose that are essentially communicating the same thing.

Third session

Have all team members write down their top three purpose statements from the brainstorming notes. Now, have your team members put a dot or mark next to their top three statements on the brainstorming sheets themselves. The three statements with the most dots or marks are the top three contenders. Can any more statements be eliminated for communicating the same message?

This is where creativity comes into play. The group can either choose to vote again for the top statement or choose to create a statement that combines ideas from two or even all three of the top contenders. Clients we've worked with have taken both routes to successful statements.

Fourth session

Time to wordsmith. Gather the group and work together to make the statement concise and meaningful. The final purpose statement should be brief—no more than a couple of sentences.

We encourage you to choose your words with care, but don't let the perfect get in the way of the good. Don't spend three hours asking yourselves what "is" is!

Fifth session

Now that you have a well-written, meaningful purpose statement, what's next? You could pop it up on the website homepage and call it a day, but then the six hours the team devoted to creating it might have been better spent—and more motivating—going zip-lining together. The purpose statement becomes powerful only when you make sure you are living it and connecting others to it.

Some companies, such as Blackrock, the multinational investment management corporation, are actually designing metrics around their purpose statements and working them into the performance management system. This may be a bridge farther than you were intending to go. But consider: Is there really any better way to integrate a meaningful purpose into a culture than to develop a core set of behaviors and ensure individuals are embodying those behaviors?

The key here is that the purpose creates connection and alignment, and the more ways you can work the purpose into the organizational identity, the more intrinsically motivated your workforce will be.

Moving from Purpose to Action

The next step is marketing the purpose within the organization. Hold focus group meetings to share the process the team used to develop the purpose. Now ask other employees to identify when they feel most connected to the purpose and what specific actions the entire organization can take to represent and embody this purpose.

Now it's time to identify ways to keep the conversation going. When the conversation about purpose ceases, so does its value. Can you hold quarterly nominations for the most purpose-driven employee? Or hold a semi-annual purpose summit to discuss how the organization can embody the purpose even more?

Don't forget what The Work Foundation study specified about the highest-performing companies: Their well-defined purpose is supported by a set of mutually reinforcing values. Let's take a look at the role both a defined competitive advantage and values play in unlocking your team's highest performance.

Chapter 5

Competitive Advantage

You are bombarded with hundreds of purchasing choices every day. From the forty items you pick up at the grocery store to the bank where you deposit your money and even the daycare you choose for your children, you make constant decisions about how to best trade money for desired outcomes.

You base your purchasing decisions on many different factors, including loyalty, convenience, prestige, or frugality. When parents make the decision to purchase organic rather than conventional produce, they may feel that organic produce is an advantageous purchase for their family, the planet, the farmer, or all three. Other consumers who share this worldview about the benefits of organic produce will seek it out, consistently forgoing conventional carrots for their organic brethren.

For many reasons organic produce often costs more than conventional. Sometimes the farm is smaller and can't exploit massive economies of scale, and pest management can be more labor intensive and therefore more expensive. On the upside, organically raised produce is often touted as being more flavorful than its conventional counterpart. The price disparity may change in time, but currently, those who purchase organic fruits and vegetables make a conscious choice to spend more money for certain desired outcomes: more flavor, less pesticide use, perceived environmental benefits, and even a closer relationship to smaller, local farms.

Farmers who grow organic produce market the organic aspect as a specific differentiator to their target consumer. While not every consumer is willing to pay more for organic, a certain market of consumers is most definitely prepared, even excited, to do so.

Successful organic produce companies have already identified Whole Foods loyalists as part of their target market. They know what type of desired outcomes these loyalists seek in a trip to the grocery store. The produce companies have an idea of their income, priorities, and buying habits. This omniscience may seem intrusive, but it actually allows the farmers to continually offer products that result in produce delight. The targeted consumers are willing to part with precious dollars because they are continually offered produce that supports a sustainable food system and ensures that their dinner parties are a smashing success.

What Exactly is Strategy?

The ability to garner brand loyalty and consistent purchasing through differentiation is the essence of strategy. Strategy is often defined as a *sustainable competitive advantage*. In "What Is Strategy?" Michael Porter—Harvard professor, revered business author, and anointed strategy demigod—sums up years of thought leadership in one paragraph: "A company can outperform rivals only if it can establish a difference that it can preserve. It must deliver greater value to customers or create comparable value at a lower cost, or do both. The arithmetic of superior profitability then follows: delivering greater value allows a company to charge higher average unit prices; greater efficiency results in lower average unit costs."[22]

Most teams will need to know their organization's competitive advantage as defined by Michael Porter. However, even if profit is not the ultimate goal, competitive advantage is a crucial determination for every team. Teams compete with others for the scarce resources needed to meet their ultimate objectives. Here are some examples:

- To reach its community impact objective, a nonprofit, volunteer-based organization must clearly communicate that volunteering for them will result in higher personal satisfaction than volunteering for other, similar nonprofits.

- A team within a larger organization pushing for a new internal initiative must be able to communicate why this initiative will result in the highest ROI out of all the other potential labor, time, and equipment investments.

- An athletic team will only dominate its competition by honing and leveraging its strengths, then attracting athletes who fit the model of its defined competitive advantage.

Any team seeking to leverage resources such as time or money toward a final objective needs to understand how best to leverage its strengths to achieve that objective. Competitive advantage is the final piece in the foundation for your team's best performance. The purpose gives the team the "reason to be," the values define how the team will work together to achieve greatness, and the competitive advantage identifies the strengths that will be used to reach the main objectives.

We have had clients who question the necessity of defining a competitive advantage for change efforts such as cultural transformation or performance management redesign. We always recommend defining all three pieces of the foundation because no matter how effective the culture or how agile the leadership, a team simply cannot deliver its highest performance without first defining its purpose, values, and competitive advantage.

In a marketplace where millions of products, services, and donation opportunities vie for your own scarce resources, why would you choose to spend your hard-earned income on anything that didn't deliver specific value to your life? You wouldn't. If organic-loving parents saw two bunches of carrots, with one bunch priced $1.00 higher and no clear advantage listed, are they likely to purchase the higher-priced carrots? No. But they are willing to spend more for carrots that offer a clearly defined advantage.

For any team to achieve its ultimate objective of increased sales, profitability, fundraising, or athletic achievement, knowing and showing its differentiation—what makes it special—is imperative.

How do you go about identifying your competitive advantage? The following process will walk you through, step-by-step, how to define what you do best and why.

Take Action: Defining Competitive Advantage

The team

As in the previous two exercises, the team should include all founders, the team or organization leader, and a representative of the organization's guiding coalition, with a maximum of seven people. Representatives of different functions and levels of management are needed for diversity of perspective and for organizational buy-in later.

Hardware needed

- At least one easel with a giant notepad, preferably with adhesive on the back
- Markers for brainstorming on the notepad

Exercise outline

Homework: Give each team member this list of questions to consider and conduct customer-based research on:

- Who are the customers who ultimately make the decisions to purchase or give their time to our products/services?

- Describe the ideal customer in detail, including the customer's needs, challenges, and reasons for seeking out our product or service.

- Describe what problem our product or service fixes for this ideal customer.

- What is most valuable about our product or service?

- Is the value we offer financial, emotional, or both?

- What is our specific target market?

First session

At the first meeting, the team will share their research and analysis, one question at a time. After discussion, the team should decide on a best answer for each question, or whether to research additional questions. (Note: the best answer is not necessarily the most common answer.) Given the number of team members and the disparity of answers, this work may take more than one session.

Second session

Use the following guidelines and template developed by Doug Staymen, Associate Dean for MBA Programs and Associate Professor of Marketing at Cornell University's Johnson Graduate School of Management, to generate a competitive positioning statement. Thanks to Mr. Staymen, defining your competitive advantage has never been so easy.

Staymen's guidelines for good positioning statements

1. It is simple, memorable, and tailored to the target market.

2. It provides an unmistakable and easily understood picture of your brand that differentiates it from your competitors.

3. It is credible, and your brand can deliver on its promise.

4. Your brand can be the sole occupier of this particular position in the market—you can own it.

5. It helps you evaluate whether or not marketing decisions are consistent with and supportive of your brand.

6. It leaves room for growth. [23]

Template for writing a positioning statement

Here's a basic template for writing a positioning statement:

For [*insert target market*], the [*insert brand*] is the [*insert point of differentiation*] among all [*insert frame of reference*] because [*insert reason to believe*].

Staymen recommends Amazon's branding statement from 2001, when the company focused primarily on book sales, as an example of a clear, competitive positioning statement: "For World Wide Web users who enjoy books, Amazon.com is a retail bookseller that provides instant access to over 1.1 million books. Unlike traditional book retailers, Amazon.com provides a combination of extraordinary convenience, low prices and comprehensive selection."

Third session

Now that you have defined your competitive advantage and created a clear competitive positioning statement, it's time to take a comprehensive look at your marketing messages and material to ensure they align with your positioning statement.

Odds are, some of your material and sales pitches will need to be revised to bring them up to date.

In transforming your team's culture into a culture of accountability, the foundation provides the clearest possible roadmap for exactly how team members will achieve success.

One of the questions we always include in our team performance assessment is, "what sets your organization apart from the competition?" It's extremely common for responses to vary wildly within a team. This means that the team is marketing itself to potential clients or volunteers inconsistently. And what follows from that is delivery of product, service, or experience that is also completely inconsistent. When team members are not representing the team's strengths with a united front, the marketing messages become diluted and weak, putting the team in an equally weak position to compete for the scarce time and money they seek to reach their goals.

Let's move now to the third key aspect of the foundation: a defined set of core values.

Chapter 6

Values

By defining your purpose and your competitive advantage, you have begun to define your team's culture. As *Firms of Endearment* defines it, *culture* is your team's "psychosocial infrastructure. It embodies the shared set of values, assumptions and perspectives that draws members of the organization together into a tight-knit, smoothly operating team dedicated to common purposes."[24] Culture is the invisible force shaped by leadership actions and by the (stated or unstated) expectations of behavior within the team.

Culture can be intentional or unintentional. A team with an unintentional culture is often one that suffers from a lack of clear direction and a dearth of accountability. After all, if you haven't defined the behaviors you expect, it is nearly impossible to hold individuals accountable to them. The framework of an intentionally high-performance culture is a set of well-defined values backed by leaders who are comfortable with ensuring that those values are enacted and supported.

Before he became an engagement expert and the chief culture officer of Stericycle, Paul Spiegelman founded BerylHealth. As CEO of that company, he learned the power of defining his company's core principles. In a 2012 article for *Inc.* magazine, "Business Values Lead To Profits? Let's Prove It," Spiegelman wrote about his epiphany: "At some point more than fifteen years ago we defined our company purpose and core values, those behaviors that would never change no matter what else changes in our business. I started to hear employees talking about these core values in meetings and using them to guide important business decisions. That's when I realized that a code of ethics means everything to our business." [25]

Work Rules

What is the key to ensuring that values are more than just website copy—that they actually define culture? That magic ingredient, accountability. As leadership expert David Cottrell has said so succinctly, "one of the best ways to ensure that workplace values 'happen' is to treat them like work rules."[26]

Have you ever had a team member who time and again created a drag on their team through poor attitude, passive aggressive-ness, or overall lack of concern for the other team members? Quite often we have leaders come to us full of frustration over team members like this, but feeling powerless to do anything about it. "After all," they say, "I can't fire someone for a bad attitude when his work is getting done."

To that we respond, "his *work* might be getting done, but is the performance of the team suffering?" The answer is almost always yes. When an individual's job expectations include only task-oriented deliverables, it's impossible to hold team members accountable to any type of behavioral standard, essentially because no cultural standard has been outlined. This is where values offer their greatest, well, *value.*

Accountability requires clear expectations from the outset, including behavioral expectations. Performance detractors such as a disrespectful attitude, lack of reliability, and even a failure to be efficient are all behaviors that can be addressed with greater ease once a values system—the "work rules"—are defined and in place. The values then become as important as any task-oriented deliverable.

How Zappos Achieved Success with Values

Have you ever ordered a new pair of shoes from the wildly successful online merchant Zappos and noticed something like "#2: Embrace and Drive Change" printed in big bold letters on the box? Zappos is so committed to living its values that every box the company ships has one of the company's values emblazoned on the side. While this example is customer facing, it's an outgrowth of the significant emphasis Zappos places on having its employees embody the company's core values at all times. A tour through the Zappos company website brings you to a core values page, which states, "[Our core values] are reflected in everything we do and every interaction we have. Our core values are always the framework from which we make all of our decisions."[27]

During its most explosive growth period, Zappos founder and CEO Tony Hsieh was trying to handpick each employee himself. Not only did this take up precious strategic time, but he also found that he was struggling to hire (and then manage) in a consistent way to ensure an enduring culture of "Delivering WOW Through Service."

The company's internal counsel recommended that the company develop a list of values to define the company's culture, and then leverage the list for hiring and managing decisions. Hseih wrote *Delivering Happiness* about the Zappos company culture, and in it he explains how critical it is to make values a part of the team fabric:

A lot of corporations have "values" or "guiding principles," but the problem is that they're usually very lofty sounding and they read like a press release that the marketing department put out. A lot of times, an employee might learn of them on day 1 of orientation, but then the values just end up being part of a meaningless plaque on the wall of a corporate lobby.

We wanted to make sure that didn't happen with our core values. We wanted a list of committable core values that we were willing to hire and fire on. If we weren't willing to do that, then they weren't really "values."

[...]when new employees join the company, they are required to sign a document stating that they have read the core values document and understand that living up to the core values is part of their job expectation.[28]

Zappos has sought to differentiate itself from the competition through its customer service, and it has ensured that its values support the behaviors that create a culture that in turn supports the company's competitive advantage. Zappos therefore attracts talent that sustains this culture and further builds the competitive advantage.

When you first considered the importance of organizational values, did your thoughts conjure up work expectations that guide hiring and firing? For many, the idea of culture-defining "work rules" is far from the definition of organizational values that first comes to mind. If this was the case for you, we encourage you to consider that by leveraging values as job expectations, you can give your team members a clear road map for their success. You wouldn't expect individuals to be high performing without clear expectations of their assigned tasks and deliverables, so how can you expect them to model the culture you are trying to build without communicating exactly what that looks like?

As noted in our discussion of purpose, all individuals bring their own motivations and core values to work. By being transparent about the purpose and core values of the organization, you appeal to those who naturally align with the organization, securing stronger buy-in and commitment from the day they're hired. Working for an organization that honors values that are wildly differing and even contradictory from your own can be stressful and disengaging. Trying to fit in can feel disingenuous. Employers that make values a strong part of the brand actually leverage their performance strengths and deep beliefs about their work as marketing tools to attract high-performing talent.

Winning the Right Way

The Work Foundation cited "mutually reinforcing values" as a critical component of the highest-performing companies because the values define the "how" in the question "how are we going to achieve our purpose and goals?" The values create the psychological framework within which team members perform. Think of it this way: A team not held accountable may choose any path to achieve their purpose and goals, ethical or not. A team operating without clear values, purpose, or accountability may even take a short-term approach to growth, risking the organization's long-term future by sacrificing quality, profits, or customer relationships.

On the other hand, a team with a lofty purpose and audacious goals that is held accountable to acting ethically, with integrity and respectfulness, will be much more likely to create long-term success and a culture others want to be a part of.

When your team's purpose and values are defined, it's much easier to identify the root causes of performance issues as they arise. Remember, values lead to behaviors, which build a culture and sustain a competitive advantage. Like a grading rubric used to evaluate student performance, values give your team a crucial vocabulary to use when behaviors are not aligning with the culture and, as a result, performance is less than expected.

Using Values to Evaluate Progress

Let's take a look at how values can help identify problems with performance when they do arise. We had been working with a medium-sized construction client for over a year when it became apparent that the team was still not achieving the performance it knew was possible. The team had improved in many ways, but projects weren't as profitable as initially planned, client relationships were yielding inconsistent outcomes, and team members felt an overall lack of focus, which was leading to disengagement.

We performed a very simple exercise with the leadership team, which revealed a deep well of knowledge that enabled the team to pinpoint the root cause of the performance issues. We began the exercise by listing on a whiteboard the company's five values: quality, accuracy, efficiency, innovation, and respectfulness.

We then asked each individual on the team to rate the company's performance in each of these values on a scale of one to ten and write the number down. Participants shared their ratings, and when the ratings were averaged, a clear picture emerged: Four of the five values had average ratings in the high eights and nines. Only one had an average rating in the low sixes: efficiency.

This wasn't a scientific measurement by any means; it was simply a way of taking the company's pulse within the context of their culture-defining values. As the numbers were averaged, people began to nod silently.

A project manager spoke up: "It feels like we don't have any particular way of doing things; it's slightly different every time. Also, there are some pretty major gaps in information between the estimators and the field."

Then another project manager added: "I'm never quite clear on exactly who needs to approve what and when. It feels like we are really inefficient compared to what we could be. We don't really have any formal processes anymore, and it means we are all doing things our own way, which might not be the best way."

Finally the quietest and most reserved individual in the group spoke: "Our quality is amazing, we blow everyone else away. If we could increase our efficiency, it would take our accuracy and quality to even a whole other level, that is where we are falling down."

Because the team had already agreed on the values it wanted to be defined by, team members were able to quickly identify which area was lapsing and what it was costing them. The team had already agreed that it wanted to be efficient and that each value mutually reinforced the others. Now the team had a clear vocabulary they could use to easily identify what was in need of performance improvement. The team agreed that day to identify, design, and implement four critical processes to improve efficiency company-wide as soon as possible.

Now it's time for your team or organization to define its values. This exercise can vary slightly depending on the size of the team or organization. We have included the appropriate options in the exercise description. Although it may seem more efficient to have the team leader list five values and ask everyone if they agree, the values won't hold meaning for everyone else. To be successful, this process requires the spirit of inclusiveness, patience, and, yes, fun!

Take Action: Defining Values

The team

As in the purpose exercise, the team chosen for this exercise should include all founders, the team or organization leader, and a representative of the organization's guiding coalition, with a maximum of seven people. Representatives of different functions and levels of management are needed for diversity of perspective and organizational buy-in later.

Hardware needed

- At least one easel with a giant notepad, preferably with adhesive on the back
- Markers for brainstorming on the notepad
- Access to a search engine

Exercise outline

Preparation homework

Give each team member this list of questions to consider:

- What does our organization stand for?
- How do we want to treat clients, partners, and each other?
- What do we want to be known for?
- What do we look like when we look our best?
- How do we act in a way that sustains our competitive advantage?

Before meeting, have your team members create a list of the seven values they feel define the team or organization's highest-performing culture. Remember that values such as efficiency and quality are easily tied to performance, but values such as openness, accountability, WOW! service, and curiosity also create the culture that enables a team to reach full performance potential.

We always encourage team members to get online and search for values lists. There are so many resources available to help with this process, and using the lists to spark ideas tends to be very efficient.

Another way to begin this process for an entire organization is to have team leaders hold focus groups with multiple smaller teams from the organization. With printed values lists, the teams can together identify up to ten recommended values to take back to the core team. This method gets many more employees involved early for stronger buy-in and achieves more organizational representation in the choosing of the values.

First session

Gather the team and list the values collected from individuals or focus groups on the giant easel. As you go through the values, make a notation next to those that were suggested more than once. This will help you track which ones were popular with team members.

Now, go through the list and identify any values that are similar enough that one or the other can be deleted from the list. For example, often one person recommends honesty and another person recommends integrity. In most cases, the group chooses to keep integrity in the running because they feel it encompasses honesty, but embodies even more. These are the types of distinctions that can help narrow the list to fewer than twenty words.

Prior to the next meeting, have everyone consider the full list of potential values and identify their top five.

Second session

Have your team members share their top five values. From these top-five lists a clear set of core values usually emerges. Starting with the seven most-recommended values, facilitate a discussion to come up with the top five to seven values. More than seven values can become unwieldy to remember as a team member. And remember that just because a particular value didn't place in the top seven, it could still shoot to the top in the course of meaningful discussion. Engage in open dialogue about the choices. As in the purpose exercise, allow for questioning and conversation without letting the perfect get in the way of the good.

Definition homework

Assign everyone a value to define. Trying to define each value from scratch in a team setting will literally take days. A much more efficient process that ends with the same high quality is to have individuals develop a foundational definition for a value, then have the team work together to fine tune the definitions.

Definitions should be no more than one or two sentences (preferably just one) and should make clear to any team member what behaviors this value requires.

Third and fourth sessions

Use these two sessions to fine-tune the values and their definitions. Don't try to tackle all the definitions in one meeting; this process takes time—you may even need to schedule an additional meeting to finish it.

Fifth session

Create a plan for sharing the proposed values with the entire organization. Zappos spent almost a year on this process, holding conversations and gathering input from the company's employees. Not every team needs to spend that amount of time, but by sharing the proposed list with the organization and being open to improvements or changes, you are showing the employees that you truly care about their perspective and are building a meaningful list to last.

Gather feedback, finalize

Once you have gathered organizational feedback, finalize the list accordingly.

Moving from Values to Action

Just as you did with the purpose statement, create a marketing plan for the values. Share the values with the organization and identify ways to keep the conversation going. You can include a "values moment" in monthly team meetings, in which someone shares a story of representing the values. You can include them in marketing material and even focus monthly coaching sessions around one particular value. Values should not just be a plaque on a wall. Finding ways to incorporate the organization's purpose and values in interesting ways so they are constantly present for the team is a powerful first step towards creating culture.

Next, hold conversations with team members about what the purpose and values mean specifically for different functions. This helps solidify how team members will "walk the talk."

We cannot stress enough the importance of keeping purpose and values front and center in team members' minds and in the team's daily conversations. It can be tempting to think of purpose and values as self-sustaining frameworks that will continue to guide behavior on their own for years to come. This is a major mistake many teams make.

Think of it this way: If there were no police or justice system to enforce laws, would the actual written laws themselves even matter? No—individual motivations would take over. Don't let your values or work rules become meaningless. Make sure that when it comes to managing performance, values are considered job expectations.

Now that you have defined your team's purpose, values, and competitive advantage, you have built the solid foundation upon which the team can build the rest of the bridge to improved performance. Your team now knows exactly why what they do is important, how they will reach their goals, and what specific strengths they have that their competitors lack. Armed with this knowledge, your team is now prepared to focus on the next step toward sustainable and spectacular success.

Part III

Organizational Performance

Chapter 7

Line of Sight

Robyn had devoted her career to cash flow, working in her firm's accounts receivable department for more than twenty-five years. She developed her processes and working habits in her first two years on the job and was never given a compelling reason to change them. She manually calculated complex invoices, mailed them at the post office, and relied on persuasiveness and long-term relationships to ensure receivables were collected on time and in the form of checks, as she hadn't yet given any thought to electronic payments.

- Since Robyn first accepted her position decades ago, client pay practices and cash management tools had changed dramatically: Clients now regularly requested invoices be emailed so they could pay via wire transfer.

- Robyn's managers lobbied for her to adopt a new cloud invoicing system so they could eliminate the time she spent manually creating billings.

- Client payments by check were taking longer and longer as they increasingly turned to paperless systems. What once took fifteen days to pay now often took sixty days or longer.

Let's face it, Robyn was an institution. Her coworkers felt that she *owned* the accounts receivable department and no amount of subtle lobbying was going to get her to change. Think back to our anatomy lesson and remember the basal ganglia, your personal habit keeper. Robyn's behaviors were deeply etched into her brain, and no one had yet created a strong enough sense of urgency to compel her to reconsider her long-held habits.

Then Robyn's company underwent changes. With new leadership on the executive team and a new strategy that was yielding significant growth through bigger clients, Robyn found herself under a lot of pressure to change her ways. But she was having a very hard time seeing herself in these newly proposed accounts receivable systems, and her amygdala was triggering her fight response big time. Dour expressions, curt responses, and passive aggressive emails were becoming par for the course.

The team knew it was time to either coach Robyn up to the new level of performance or coach her out of her position. The company was quickly outgrowing its current cash management processes, and the lack of consistent cash flow was costing thousands per month in interest expenses from the bank.

We were brought in during an effort to review the organization's overall approach to growth and culture, and one of the new executives, Mike, pulled us aside to ask for some advice. He didn't want to sour morale by firing Robyn, but he didn't know how to get through to her.

We coached Mike on how to have a conversation with Robyn around line of sight, which would become the defining performance framework for their entire organization. *Line of sight* is a research-proven technique for improving team and organizational performance that was developed by Dr. Wendy Boswell, a professor and researcher at Texas A&M University.[29] The technique is called line of sight because it describes the ability to see clearly the direct link between individual goals and effort and the overall goals of the organization. Many employees we have consulted with could not describe how their work directly contributed to organizational success, leaving them without a strong sense of purpose or motivation to reach their goals. Dr. Boswell defines the technique as the combination of two factors: "Line of sight is an employee's understanding of the organization's goals and what actions are necessary to contribute to those objectives. To translate strategic goals into tangible results, employees must not only understand the organization's strategy, but must also accurately appreciate the actions aligned with realizing that strategy."[30]

A $30,000 Breakthrough

Six months after our conversation with Mike, Robyn had left the sour expressions behind and was learning to adapt to new processes and an entirely new set of goals. What changed? Mike learned how to leverage line of sight to create the commitment and intrinsic motivation needed for Robyn to want to change her habits.

To kick-start the process, we encouraged Mike to learn more about Robyn's motivations and how she saw herself contributing to the organization's success. All hardworking, committed employees see their efforts as critical to the team in some way, sometimes it's just not the *right way*. This was the case with Robyn.

Robyn explained to Mike that it was her responsibility to collect the money from clients and track every dollar through the system, which she could do with her long-held process. She also admitted she was afraid to use a computer system because she might struggle to learn it, and because if it was so efficient, it might make her job obsolete.

Before talking with Robyn, Mike prepared a very crucial calculation. He calculated precisely how much profit the organization would retain if the accounts receivable operations were automated, run through wire transfers, and collected more aggressively. He showed Robyn that if each of these changes had been in place sooner, Robyn would not only have saved interest expenses for the organization, but she would also have made profit for the company from the interest *earned* on their much higher daily cash balance.

Mike described to Robyn how crucial profit was at that moment to the company's growth strategy, and how without the profit, the company would need to tap into the bank's line of credit day in and day out, making growth very expensive. He shared with her the profit goal for the company in the coming year and showed her she could make a difference of $30,000! She alone could transform the cash position by learning some new behaviors and processes.

Mike successfully used line of sight to link Robyn's behaviors to the overall company's success. Robyn had never seen so clearly how her actions and goals affected the team's overall success. Knowing that she had the leadership team's support to learn these new behaviors, Robyn agreed to take on the challenge of learning new, automated processes. She knew it wouldn't be easy, but she was determined to be the accounts receivable manager who could take credit for saving the company tens of thousands of dollars in hard-earned profit.

The Key to Line of Sight Success

Let's highlight for a moment that Robyn's line of sight didn't stop at knowing she could make a difference to the bottom line. In addition—and crucially—she knew exactly *how to change her behaviors* to amplify her strategic contribution. As Dr. Boswell explains, "An employee's understanding of the behaviors that are critical to the organization's strategic goals is more important than his or her ability to simply articulate those goals back to the managers; further, grasping how to effectively contribute is paramount. More direct one-on-one communication aimed at specifically linking employee roles and behaviors to larger organizational goals is key."[31] The key, as Dr. Boswell explains, is to ensure that line of sight is not a lofty, abstract vision along the lines of "as an employee I make a difference." A vague connection to overall team success is not going to take employees to the next level of performance. Rather, the power of line of sight is unleashed when team members know exactly how their specific behaviors and actions support targeted organizational goals.

Think back to the foundation: Remember how a clear team purpose connects individuals to something greater than themselves, sparking intrinsic motivation and leading to discretionary effort? Line of sight takes purpose even further. Armed with metrics and a clear understanding of the most effective behaviors she could undertake every day, Robyn felt empowered and emboldened to hit those goals and *become an invaluable team member*.

There is a reason employees look so thrilled when you present them with kudos—they feel valued and *valuable*. When employees know explicitly how their daily output contributes to team success, the highest performers will stop at nothing to ensure they continue to be seen as valuable. You have given them the playbook and the right coaching and challenged them to go win at their job. Like Robyn, they won't want to let you down.

Strategic Alignment

We consultants throw around a lot of jargon. It's a symptom of reading way too many issues of the *Harvard Business Review*. While all the research we do benefits the teams we work with, we sometimes catch ourselves using terms like *psychometric*, *meta-analysis*, and *synergy*, which, we get it, often sound either pretentious or ridiculous.

Strategic alignment might also sound like business magazine jargon, but I assure you that this is one term you want to add to your vocabulary. The federal Office of Personnel Management defines *strategic alignment* concisely as "having a human capital strategy aligned with mission, goals, and organizational objectives."[32] While our earlier discussion of alignment outlined the benefits of using purpose to align the team with *intrinsic motivation*, alignment through a distinct *strategy* means every team member knows the ultimate destination, the route to get there, and everyone's role in the effort. Pairing purpose alignment with strategic alignment yields a powerful combination of passionately motivated individuals who understand exactly how to execute their part in a successful plan.

Think back to the example of Robyn. Before Mike created line of sight for Robyn, she was operating from her own objectives and her own set of rules. Once the company had a clear purpose and set of goals for itself, it could easily break those goals down into individual goals for employees. If all employees hit their individual goals, then the company can celebrate success as all those individual goals aggregate into one large win.

This is how strategic alignment works. When you first drop this term on your team, excuse them for looking at you like you, too, have been reading too many *Harvard Business Review*s. Then explain that there really is no better way than strategic alignment to ensure that all your team members' goals and actions are pointing in the same direction as overall team success.

This process removes the frustration of competing priorities, mismatched goals, and even costly counterproductive behaviors. Imagine if your team members were aligned around a clear purpose and a set of explicit values, but their goals were created in silos without any regard to the aims of other teams.

Building the foundation was the first step in anchoring your team or organization in a shared vision. It's now time to outline the tangible goals and key performance indicators that will influence behaviors day in and day out.

Let's take a second to recap what we've just learned. Line of sight and strategic alignment are very closely linked, but it's important to note that they aren't the same thing. You need both to be successful, but as you lead your team through the process, you will be using these terms in subtle, yet important ways.

Think of them this way: *Strategic alignment* is the process through which you ensure all team members have defined goals and actions that will support overall team success. *Line of sight* is the outcome of the strategic alignment process; you know line of sight is present when all of your team members can describe how their goals and actions support overall team success.

By starting with the process of strategic alignment and then ensuring that your team has crystal clear line of sight, you will have positioned yourselves as a much more efficient and effective group.

Thanks to Dr. Boswell's research on line of sight, we know that the highest-performing teams have achieved clear line of sight. But of course it wasn't enough for us just to know *that* it works; our insatiable curiosity meant we wanted to know *why*.

Combining with Purpose for a Powerful One-Two Punch

It turns out line of sight affects team members in almost *exactly the same ways* purpose does. In fact, the two reinforce each other. If purpose explains why a team is going to give their all for a common goal, line of sight is the battle plan for how they will achieve the goal.

Just like purpose, line of sight facilitates the development of two areas crucial for performance: intrinsic motivation and alignment. These two old friends might look familiar, since we just spent a considerable number of pages describing how crucial both intrinsic motivation and alignment are to success. Both of these attributes are themes that run through this entire book. You don't need a PhD to know that a motivated, aligned team is going to be higher performing than an unmotivated and completely disorganized team, and many of the tools we offer in this book work specifically to increase both motivation and alignment.

Just as compound interest is one of the most powerful forces in financial gain, compounding motivation using purpose and line of sight leads to an unstoppable team. As Dr. Boswell explains, "the more employees believe in the strategic goals of the organization, the greater their line of sight and the more likely they are to pursue those objectives."[33]

Robyn was already deeply committed to her company and its purpose. Once she was given the opportunity to serve the purpose in a more meaningful and explicit way that both increased her value as an employee and the chances of organizational success, she was willing to change her own behaviors and learn new habits to achieve a new set of goals.

When it comes to alignment, purpose enables the team to effectively pool their efforts toward a shared vision, while line of sight serves to remove the lingering inefficiencies that can stall a team's success.

A 2013 study, "Performance Improvement in High-Performance Organizations," cosponsored by the Institute for Corporate Productivity and the International Society for Performance Improvement, found conflicting goals and objectives were the *number one* barrier to high performance.[34] Conflicting goals and objectives signal a lack of strategic alignment. When team members' goals and objectives don't meld to create overall success, they can instead damage any chance of long-term success.

With more than forty percent of both high-performance and low-performance organizations naming conflicting goals and objectives as their number one barrier to success, it's clear that a lack of strategic alignment prevents even the best organizations from achieving their potential. The Performance Improvement in High-Performance Organizations study shows that "receiving different messages about what needs to be accomplished and when has an immobilizing effect on employees. It also presents them with a quandary of who to go to for a decision. Mixed messages will slow down the entire initiative."[35] Think back for a second to how confusing it was as a child to get mixed messages from different parents. You were either very confused or you learned quickly who to manipulate for another cookie. Neither of these behaviors—paralysis or manipulation—are ingredients for a high-performing team.

Make sure they aren't holding your team back by outlining a clear strategy for success and communicating objectives consistently.

Now that you've introduced your team to the concept of strategic alignment, you need to be able to back up your recommendations with action. We're going to walk you through the basics of the strategic alignment process so you can achieve line of sight and remove any conflicting goals and objectives that may be inhibiting your success.

Take Action: Aligning People With Strategy

1. Have a strategy.

Before you can align people with your strategy, you need to have one. This is why your foundation is so important. Only when your entire organization knows your victory plan will they understand their role in it.

An organization's strategic plan will include its specific competitive advantage, target market, pricing, and an analysis of competition. A nonprofit's strategic plan will include its specific competitive advantage, target client market, funding target market, and an assessment of current resources.

2. Define your goals.

Begin outlining your long-term and short-term goals. In a turnaround situation, as in the case study at the end of this section, a team may have only six months to reach their goals. Most teams, however, should be in the habit of setting annual goals and even longer term strategic goals that are three to five years out.

3. Create your scorecard.

An important distinction to make is the difference between a goal and a key performance indicator (KPI). A goal is your desired final outcome, while a KPI is the metric we use to measure performance and progress. KPIs can be used on a daily, weekly, or monthly basis to track progress toward goals. An example of a goal is earning $300 million in annual revenue. An example of a KPI is the number of qualified sales leads generated per month.

A scorecard of balanced KPIs helps you monitor success as you take your team's performance to the next level. In the next chapter, we will outline how to identify the right balanced scorecard for your team.

4. Apply the scorecard to various departments and individuals.

Ready for more exciting strategic-alignment vocabulary? At this point in the process, you undertake what is called *cascading*. Like a waterfall that breaks into smaller waterfalls before reaching its destination, you work to break goals into smaller pieces and give ownership of those pieces to each department or individual on your team.

Remember how Robyn was able to contribute to her company's overarching profitability goal by making it possible to earn $30,000 in interest? Mike managed to successfully cascade the larger profit goal down to a specific goal and specific actions Robyn could take to help ensure organizational success.

The cascading process usually takes one to three years. A large team can be easily overwhelmed by a new set of goals and KPIs if these have been foreign concepts until now.

At the end of the cascading process, each individual on your team should be responsible for a blend of no more than five strategic goals and KPIs.

5. Enjoy line of sight. Review at least annually.

When the individuals on your team can describe how their goals and actions support the overall goals and actions of the organization, you'll know you have successfully created the line of sight needed to increase motivation and alignment.

As with any other system we recommend in this book, there is unfortunately no autopilot button. If a system such as a strategic network of goals is put into place then left to its own devices, it's actually being left to its own demise. Systems and goals do not a high-performing team make. Only when combined with accountability and crucial regular check-ins do strategically aligned goals increase a team's motivation and alignment for its best performance.

Don't ever set it and forget it. In the next chapter you'll learn more about the right frequency for reviewing important measurements.

Common Questions, Actionable Answers

In theory, line of sight is (no pun intended) pretty straightforward. In practice, however, lots of valid concerns arise. If left unaddressed, these concerns can prevent leaders from moving forward with the effort to increase strategic alignment. Keep in mind that for every concern that can come up around creating line of sight a solution most definitely exists. Here are the three most common concerns we have encountered when introducing line of sight:

1. I have three levels of leadership in my organization, and this is our first year determining strategic goals and KPIs. Should I cascade those goals down to individuals this first year?

This is an important question, and one that has a slightly different answer depending on the team. For an organization that has never had goals or KPIs in place, it's wise to take one to three years cascading goals down from the organizational to the individual level. The cascading can be done in phases, with goals cascading down one more leadership level each successive year until every individual in the organization has a set of goals and KPIs.

If a team has one or two leaders and a large group of individual contributors, then it is entirely appropriate to determine the overall team goals and KPIs, then cascade them down to individuals immediately or within the first year.

In a larger organization, it can also be prudent to start with a handful of functional departments and cascade down for lessons learned and immediate wins. With the system working in these initial departments, it can be even easier to introduce to a more resistant or complex department.

2. Once we have our goals and KPIs in place, how can we support line of sight throughout the year?

It is extremely important to keep goals and KPIs uppermost in mind for employees throughout the year. Line of sight motivates and aligns only if team members consider how their actions and goals are supporting overall success on a daily basis.

As you'll read later, we always recommend to clients that all their employees have the benefit of a monthly one-on-one check-in with their leader to track KPIs and build a relationship based on regular, open dialogue. By tracking KPIs monthly, a leader and individual can work together to correct any performance concerns long before an annual goal is missed. Just as crucial, these check-ins give the leader the opportunity to offer congratulations and kudos to team members who are performing well and acting as a great example to the team.

Dr. Boswell recommends two more ways of supporting line of sight: holding two different types of team meetings.[36] Recall that line of sight is most effective when employees can describe how both their goals *and* their actions support overall organizational success. Interestingly, it turns out that optimally supporting line of sight with goals and line of sight with actions requires two different types of meetings.

The organization-wide meeting, which brings teams, departments, and functions together to share strategic goals and direction, is the best forum for enhancing line of sight for goals. During this meeting, leadership can describe clear links between annual organizational goals and annual department or functional goals. This forum also helps break down functional silos as different departments see firsthand how other departments are supporting overall success and how the organization relies on each and every team.

The department-wide meeting is the best way leadership can enhance line of sight around specific actions. Think about it: When a team gathers to discuss their impending success, the discussion is often centered on what specific actions are most effective for long-term success. In this forum, the entire team can learn from one another which actions are best to undertake on a regular basis for individual, departmental, and organizational success.

3. I have members of my team who are completely against goals and measurement. They tell me they know what they need to do and they get it done. They are threatening to leave if I implement goals and KPIs. How do I handle this?

This is one of the hardest questions we get on a regular basis. Certain individuals have a visceral fight, flight, or freeze response to measurement. First of all, it's critical to acknowledge that your team members may see measurement as a real threat. It's new and scary, and they are no doubt worried about not being able to undertake the actions or meet the goals that will support the organization's new definition of success.

This fear usually arises from one of two scenarios. The first involves a team member who is very attached to a flexible work setting without many rules, goals, or a high level of accountability. This may stem from how the individual was raised, or it may be that at some point during this person's career, he or she learned being considered a success was easier if no goals were set for them. Many team members pick up what Marshall Goldsmith calls "success strategies" that don't actually serve them as they need to grow and evolve, hence the title of Goldsmith's bestseller: *What Got You Here Won't Get You There.*[37]

The second scenario involves the team member who had been part of a team that abused goals and KPIs in a way that created fear, unhealthy competition, and unethical behavior. There's a reason for the saying "we become what we measure." When line of sight is implemented the right way, it builds on an organization's competitive advantage, purpose, and core values to reinforce a strong culture. When used incorrectly, and without the foundation described in the previous section, measurement can become a substitute for leadership and an excuse for actions that break down trust and ethics.

In either scenario, the approach to supporting team members through the implementation of strategic alignment is the same. First, make sure you understand their concerns by asking lots of open-ended questions that will get you to the root of their worry. Then work to build trust around the system by offering support, coaching, and assurance that the measurements will at first be observations with no judgment. Initially, measurements should be treated as a trial run and calibration process. Make it clear that no one will be disciplined or fired for not meeting goals as the team formalizes the measurement process over a specified time period. Finally, be sure to explain how the measurement process actually helps the organization recognize the employee's contribution more clearly. As in Robyn's case, your team member will now understand how to have a direct impact on the bottom line and the organization's long-term success.

4. I lead a team within an organization, but I don't have the authority to lead a total strategic alignment effort. I can only control what's on my team, and my organization hasn't given me any goals and KPIs. How can I ensure line of sight with my team if we don't know how to define overall success?

As you read through this book, recognize that everything is scalable. Just because your organization has not given you a clear set of goals or KPIs doesn't mean that they don't have an idea of what they are expecting from your team.

Start by asking your leader some questions that can help you determine what success looks like for your team. See if your leader can give you a definition of success, and with it some goals for your team to achieve. Then work with your team to translate those goals into KPIs that you can monitor throughout the year. If you have an exceedingly challenging leader who won't work with you to define success, then it's time for you and your team to have a discussion around what success means to you. Remember that line of sight increases your team's performance whether the overall organization has implemented strategic alignment or not.

If you can build buy-in from your team to create a balanced set of goals and KPIs and then support each other in reaching success, your team will be showing up every day with increased motivation and alignment that organizational leadership will surely notice.

Every system in this book takes your team closer and closer to a culture of accountability. By establishing a strong foundation for the team, with a competitive advantage, purpose, and core values, you built a solid framework to support a conversation about accountability. Now, with line of sight, accountability not only becomes even more crucial, but easier. It is next to impossible to create a culture of accountability with vague expectations.

When a system of strategic alignment is in place, all team members have clear goals and KPIs that help them gauge their success throughout the year. This system makes it easier than ever for organizational leadership to monitor individual progress and offer the coaching and calibration to guarantee individual and team success.

Creating line of sight is a goal that must be approached with patience and a willingness to commit to identifying the goals and actions that define success for your team. Some leaders are loathe to define goals for fear that not hitting them puts them in a weakened position. The best teams in the world miss their goals and learn from the experience to come back stronger. The vast majority of mediocre teams across the globe don't bother with goals and never truly reach their potential. Which type of team would you rather lead?

Checklist for Creating Line of Sight

- Ensure that your team or organization has a set of long-term goals and shorter term KPIs that align directly with the organization's foundation.

- Determine your team's or organization's measurement maturity and cascade accordingly. If the team or organization has been measuring performance against goals for some time, ensure that you have strategic, department, and individual goals. If goals and measurement are new concepts, stick with high-level strategic goals initially.

- Communicate ad nauseam. You will have created line of sight successfully only when individuals at all levels of the organization are able to articulate how their work supports the team's or organization's overall strategy and long-term goals.

Chapter 8

What Gets Measured...

Have you ever been part of an organization that prized sales above all else? Maybe you worked on a team where a high revenue number was the Holy Grail, and the sales team was treated like knights in shining armor. This is an example of the distortion that can come from myopic measurement.

We've all heard "what gets measured gets managed," but rarely do we think about how to measure *successfully*. The power of measurement is that it focuses near-constant effort and attention on your team's most crucial operations and outcomes. A strong foundation, comprising competitive advantage, purpose, and values, becomes worthwhile only if those elements shape behavior. By measuring performance in the form of goals and KPIs that link individuals with the foundation, you are ensuring that the right behaviors will be discussed, developed, and rewarded.

Measurement Pitfalls

Let's take a moment to look at the two major pitfalls of measurement efforts.

1. We don't have great managers or strong accountability, so we will measure *everything*.

There is a point at which measurement becomes more hindrance than help. If your employees are spending most of their time gathering data and processing reports rather than working toward their actual goals, you may have a case of measurement overload. Measurements help individuals prioritize and monitor. When everything is considered a priority and monitoring is more important than doing, measurement has lost its effectiveness. Measurement guru Dean Spitzer describes this phenomenon: "As a result of today's data collection mania, some companies have become buried in their own 'data mines.'"[38] Furthermore, measuring the wrong things or unnecessary things brings with it high costs of measurement, both in terms of actual cost and opportunity cost. Certainly there is enough real work to do today without inundating employees with needless data that confuses more than it clarifies.

2. We need cash flow and we need it now, so we will focus solely on sales and figure out the rest later.

Just as it's easy to fall into measurement overload, it can be very tempting to oversimplify. One clean energy client we worked with was growing steadily but threatened with going under due to cash-flow constraints. They had focused so much on the revenue goal that they never bothered to ensure their projects were meeting their budgeted profits. Without any attention focused on profit, projects regularly went over budget as crews hastily moved on to the next client.

The sales team was unaware of any way they had contributed to the company's precarious position; after all, they were bringing in contract after contract. However, because this firm had not yet built its foundation, they hadn't identified their competitive advantage. This in turn meant they hadn't determined their ideal client. The result of so much action without focus was that many projects were sold to less than ideal clients with very thin margins, which quickly evaporated with no project oversight.

In other organizations, an oversimplified focus on sales might mean that the sales team is treated like rock stars. Even when they are temperamental, unethical, egotistical, or unreliable, if they bring in the sales, they are placed on a pedestal. In this case, myopic measurement literally destroys the culture of a company as it completely forsakes its foundation and violates its purpose and values on a daily basis.

Neither of these approaches achieves increased accountability, motivation, or performance. By measuring too much, the measures themselves become meaningless noise. By focusing solely on sales, an organization risks sacrificing a long-term vision of success and even margins.

Performance-driving measurement takes time to develop and patience to let it evolve. It also requires testing and retesting certain measures to identify whether or not they are meaningful and eliciting the desired behaviors.

The potential risk in measuring too many things or too few of the wrong things is mitigated by adopting one of the most prized management concepts to emerge from the 1990s: the balanced scorecard.

The Balanced Scorecard

David Norton and Robert Kaplan sparked a measurement revolution in 1992 when their *Harvard Business Review* article introduced business leaders to the notion that an organization's intangible assets were just as valuable, if not at times more valuable, than its tangible assets.[39]

Yes, of course we must measure cash flow and profit, but what about employee development, brand identity, and the efficiency of our business processes? Norton and Kaplan created an excellent scorecard that balances four key areas of measurement: financial, customer, internal business process, and learning and growth.

To ensure alignment with your foundation, your team's scorecard should be a custom, high-level categorization of your goals and KPIs. It should be a natural reflection of your competitive advantage and purpose. For example, teams that offer clients a high-end experience would most likely measure profit per client, while a high-volume, low-price store might measure sales per day.

Perhaps your team should measure quality, employee engagement, or capacity building. Whichever measures you choose, Norton and Kaplan recognized that the financial measurements are the outcomes of each of the other areas of measurement. If the only time you measure your organization's success is at the end of the year, it's far too late.

By approaching your team's performance measurement in a balanced way with frequent, scheduled milestones, you give yourself the time and space to calibrate when necessary. If your customer retention ratio has taken a nosedive in quarter 2, you want to know this long before your cash begins to dry up in quarter 4.

If your organization's success depends on the competitive advantage of customer retention but you've never measured it, how can you possibly know whether your dollars spent on sales, marketing, and service are creating the highest return on investment?

We've met many leaders who rely solely on their monthly financials to gauge success and feel they are truly on top of performance measurement. It's always tough to break the news to them that the information they are reviewing is at best two months out of date and at worst a year or more. A profitable monthly financial statement typically reflects the successful billing of profitable goods and services. These goods and services were procured by customers who were first marketed to days or even years before they made their purchasing decision.

We've told these leaders that to ensure future success, they need to be aware of levels of customer engagement, conversion, and retention, not just the end result of a completed cycle. At the end of a cycle, it's harder to pinpoint and correct a problem within the process.

Keep in mind two truths:

1. Just because you are making enough cash to remain open year after year does not mean your team is living up to its potential. You are leaving cash (growth, innovation, social impact) on the table if this is your measure of success.

2. As they say on Wall Street, *past performance is not indicative of future results.* Your customers change, your competition changes, and, of course, the technology you licensed earlier this year is already out of date. The point is that leading a successful organization or team in today's marketplace requires the ability to constantly synthesize real-time information and adjust accordingly.

With the correct balanced scorecard, you have in place a system of early warning signs that will alert you that you are on track to meet your goals, fall far short of them, or crush them as your strategic alignment pays off in resplendent success.

Take Action: Your Balanced Scorecard

So, how do you choose the right scorecard for you?

1. Start with the end goal in mind.

Your financial scorecard is the first set of measurements.

2. Work backwards to identify which parts of your competitive advantage need to be measured.

If your competitive advantage is the incredible efficiency of your process, which enables a faster product turnaround time, well, you have two crucial measures right there: process efficiency and order turnaround time. If you have a cloud-based program that tracks client usage, you will want to know when usage decreases.

3. Make sure your people measure up.

The final set of measures is often the most challenging: people measures. Financial measures tend to be the easiest, with process and competitive advantage coming in a close second. People measures, however, are often intangible enough to send even the most hardened MBA running from the conference room.

Let's start with the basics: How is your employee retention? How many of your employees are taking advantage of development opportunities? How many networking events have your employees attended?

Every single type of measurement will evolve with time, but starting with the basics gives you solid data from which to make solid decisions. In the absence of data, the loudest opinion tends to win—not a great basis for sound decision making. Using a balanced scorecard arms you with data-driven assessments and information and empowers your team or organization to make real-time shifts in approach to ensure goals are met and performance continues to increase.

When Measurements Collide

Just as a team can be too focused on sales or profit with too many measurements in place, problems created by conflicting measurements can also arise. One all-too-common example of conflicting goals is asking customer service representatives to interact with as many customers as possible in a day while still offering the best customer service possible. In call centers, it's not uncommon to give employees the goal of keeping phone calls to five minutes or less in order to decrease wait times for other customers calling in. However, if an individual's performance is tied equally to this number *and* to customer service ratings, which one prevails?

Some managers might argue that this is a perfect example of a balanced approach to goals. We do agree that with excellent training and ongoing coaching, an employee may be able to offer excellent customer service within five minutes, but when an employee must decide half a dozen times a day whether to wrap up a call with a slightly dissatisfied customer or stay on the line to ensure the customer hangs up happy, which decision will the employee be rewarded for? It's very important in a case like this to clearly outline which goal takes priority. Otherwise, you end up with individual employees applying their own interpretations to the goals, which results in very inconsistent outcomes.

Remember the study conducted by the Institute for Corporate Performance and the International Society for Performance Improvement? That study found that conflicting objectives and priorities arose even in well-run teams: "Respondents from HPOs (High Performing Organizations) were nearly three times as likely as LPOs (Low Performing Organizations) to say their leaders effectively articulated the organization's strategy (goals and objectives). This enthusiasm, however, is tempered by HPOs also citing conflicting goals and objectives as a top barrier to performance improvement."[40]

The balanced scorecard is the how-to manual for guiding your strategically aligned team members to success. They know their role in the effort, they know the game plan, and they have the list of goals that explain exactly what success looks like along the way. As team leader, it will be important for you to discuss the scorecard with your team to ensure that it doesn't unintentionally cause confusion through seemingly conflicting goals.

The purpose of a balanced scorecard is to provide a holistic view of organizational and team performance. It is intended to ensure revenue and profit are not gained at the expense of quality, employee morale, or even care for the environment. A balanced scorecard inherently forces leaders and teams to identify priorities.

However, if a balanced scorecard is communicated without a clear sense of which priority is the top one, then two or more goals with seemingly equal priority can diminish each other, and measurement becomes problematic.

How Measurement Changed an Industry

A major change occurred in the construction industry in the 1980s that illustrates how two previously conflicting goals can coexist through prioritization. Before the 1980s, safety in the construction industry may have been measured, but it was a low priority. For many companies in the industry, quality, budget, profit, and schedule all trumped safety as a focus. As the Occupational Safety and Health Administration became a more prominent force and drug testing was introduced, safety slowly and steadily rose in priority.

In today's construction industry, safety statistics are so important they alone can determine whether or not a company is allowed to submit a bid for work. Every prominent construction company reached an inflection point some time in the past fifteen years. The inflection point is the precise moment when the CEO decided that his crews should choose a safe decision over a profitable one.

Are construction crews charged with ensuring safety *and* profitability? Absolutely—both are part of a balanced scorecard. But imagine a roofer faced with deciding whether to replace the damaged rope that ties him to the structure and charge the resulting overtime to the job, or to simply finish up his work on time, knowing that the probability of slipping is miniscule.

Thirty years ago, the roofer would have stayed on the roof without question. In today's industry, he would most likely be fired for doing so. Again, both profit and safety are measured, but one has a higher priority than the other. Today's successful construction companies make safety their number one priority.

Frequently the head of safety reports directly to the CEO. By clearly communicating that safety is the number one priority and then walking the talk, construction companies are safer, and more efficiently safe, than ever before.

Don't make your team guess which priority is number one. Make sure communication *and* action make priorities completely clear.

The Right Frequency

What would happen if sports teams had to wait until the end of every game to know the score? Would the teams play their best? Would they know which players to move on or off the field? Would they know when it was time to implement a riskier play?

The answer to all these questions is most likely no. It would be nearly impossible to correlate specific players or tactics with winning or losing scores, and the players wouldn't have the benefit of real-time feedback. The best sports teams have specific plays for each adversary and a strategy that can be calibrated if their opponents have new and surprising approaches.

The best team leaders have the same approach. They have an overall strategy that leverages their team's competitive advantage. That strategy leverages the strengths of certain players to produce the results outlined in the team's balanced scorecard. If the leader isn't able to gather data for real-time feedback throughout the year, the entire team is essentially just playing hard and hoping for the best. Without information, tactics become best guesses rather than informed decisions.

So, the question becomes, how often do you tally your balanced scorecard? The answer is that dreaded response you so often hear from corporate attorneys: It depends. If you review your net profit every day of the year, are you doing yourself a service or wasting your time? Most likely the five to ten minutes spent on that number is not beneficial on a daily basis.

However, spending time that way would be beneficial if your bottom line depended on a particular daily process being completed in seven minutes and with a quality score of 98 percent. If that is the case, it is mission critical that someone be watching that number daily. If you set that goal in January, yet don't know until June that your process was actually taking nine minutes with a quality score of 77 percent, it's way too late to calibrate and reach your profit goal for the year.

How frequently you check on each measure depends directly on how often relevant data for that measure are produced. Revenues and profits are often listed on a monthly financial statement, and monthly is a perfect frequency for reviewing both. If your sales cycle is six weeks, with sales closing every week, reviewing weekly conversion rates makes sense. If your sales cycle is nine months with a few sales closing every month, monthly might make sense for that review as well.

As you start to build your balanced scorecard, each measurement will have its own logical frequency. If in doubt, ask yourself how often you can feasibly collect accurate data for the measurement and then err on the side of high frequency. As you pilot gathering the data, be on the lookout for times when the data are meaningless because the review frequency is too high. You'll know then that it's time to review at a lower frequency. Just like establishing the right strategic goals and KPIs, identifying the right frequency of review is a learned skill that improves with time and experimentation.

Checklist for Ensuring High-Performance Measurement

- Ensure your goals and KPIs are not focused entirely on sales and bottom-line results.

- Create a balanced scorecard by focusing on the tangible and intangible aspects of your team that create success.

- Outline a measurement review schedule that empowers team members to make real-time decisions about performance. With timely data in hand, teams will have the information they need to modify tactics and behavior as soon as an unexpected hurdle appears.

Chapter 9

Communicating About Performance

The best advice we received about team communication came from another consultant long ago: "When, and only when, you have communicated to the point that you are sick of hearing it, everyone else is just beginning to listen." We didn't fully understand the incredible truth of this advice until much later.

This is one of the few rules we live by that doesn't come straight from a scientific journal. Years of experience have shown it to be true time after time. We were working with a CEO recently who was incredibly frustrated that an employee couldn't remember the three new strategic priorities. After all, he said, they had just been emailed out that week. Yes, you read that correctly: They had been *emailed*.

Little is more important to an organization's success than its strategic priorities. These priorities help shape every team member's behaviors in a way that results in the organization's long-term success. Unfortunately, mission-critical messages are too often delivered in emails that make *Anna Karenina seem like a quick read*, sent out as though they share the same importance as your recent purchase confirmation from Amazon.

Just think about what needs to happen in order for an employee to find the strategic outline email within the inbox jungle:

1. The employee has to actually see the email among the two hundred she received that day.

2. She then must choose to open it instead of the fifty emails with exclamation points or red flags attached.

3. Once the email is opened, the office must be silent as she carefully reads, absorbs, and processes the sacred strategic content filling her screen as she scrolls... and scrolls... and scrolls.

4. She then needs to schedule time to ponder how to translate these high-level strategic priorities into daily behaviors.

5. And finally, as her customers call with frustrations, she is assigned to three project task forces, and she begins a company recycling initiative, it's paramount that she remember these strategic priorities and carry them with her day in and day out.

Even the highest-performing team members, if they managed to find the email buried in their inbox, would assuredly not absorb and apply the strategic priorities. That's not how our brains work.

Support the New Strategic Plan

Think back to what we discussed before, and how strong a force the basal ganglia exert on our habits. In order for team members to apply new behaviors to work, they must deeply understand what those new behaviors are, contrast them mentally with the behaviors they are currently accustomed to, and find mechanisms to retrain their habits to support the new strategic plan.

One nonprofit we worked with sent out an email to all employees explaining a change in the process for filling out timecards. A simple enough message, a simple enough behavior. The human resources director thought, "Our employees read their email, and it's simple enough to understand." Did it work? Do you even have to ask? Of course not.

Employees had been filling out their timecard one way for *years*. It was second nature; they didn't even think about it anymore. When the new method was established, there was no training to help individuals absorb it, no coaching to make sure they understood how to do it properly, and no reminders about the new method when timecards were due and they needed to remember and apply the new behavior.

This left the HR director and the payroll manager scrambling to correct timesheets twice a month because more than half of them were completed incorrectly. Imagine what a stressful situation not only for HR and payroll, but also for the employees who had to make corrections quickly and manage their concerns about the accuracy of their paychecks.

This all could have been avoided by following some simple steps that support the basal ganglia in changing habits. Let's take a look at these steps.

Step 1: The Kickoff

The kickoff sets the stage for a change in behavior. A kickoff can take many forms. Essentially, it is a forum that lays the groundwork for new behaviors by setting new expectations and reviewing the specific actions and tools needed for success.

The scale and cost of a kickoff should be correlated to the impact of the change expected. If the change expected is organization-wide *and* affects the majority of goals and actions in the organization, then the kickoff should be conducted in person, include the executive team, and have an appropriate level of formality.

For something like a change in payroll process, a ten-minute mandatory webinar or an agenda item at an all-staff meeting would be entirely appropriate. The kickoff delivery method will also depend on the nature and geography of the team.

Take a second to think back a couple of chapters to the discussion of line of sight. Can you see how this type of communication approach is aligned with Dr. Boswell's recommendations? Remember, Dr. Boswell prescribed high-level strategic meetings as the best mechanism for helping individuals feel aligned and part of the organization's overall strategic goals.

Any type of large-scale kickoff for a new strategic plan, goals, or cultural change provides a rare and valuable opportunity to reinforce line of sight and boost employee performance. Be sure to take advantage of this opportunity and incorporate line of sight into the planning.

Step 2: Coaching

By the end of this book, you may never want to read or hear the word *coaching* again. If that is the case, then we'll feel we've done our job as your literary, *ahem*, coaches. Individuals with a high level of self-discipline and motivation may be able to coach themselves to new behaviors, but frankly, these types of individuals are rare.

Imagine you decided that there would be no better way to impress your kids than by learning how to play guitar. You go out and purchase a used guitar and watch YouTube videos until you've managed to pick up the basics. You have the foundational notes down and can manage to pluck out some chords. You recognize, however, that to introduce "Stairway to Heaven" into your repertoire, you would need to find someone to guide you to the next level, giving you real-time feedback on your skills and performance.

In this section of the book, we have introduced a host of behaviors that may be entirely new to employees:

- Learning how to work toward high-level strategic goals
- Translating those goals into regular, recurring actions and behaviors that drive success
- Reviewing data on a consistent basis to calibrate as necessary and ensure success

Learning how to adopt these new skills and become proficient at them is no different from picking up a guitar for the first time.

Sheer will and ambition will take you only so far. Everyone needs both support and feedback to reach a new level of performance.

Step 3: Habit-Forming Reminders

A manager can't and shouldn't be at an employee's side every day to remind them when and how to adopt new behaviors. However, that doesn't mean that employees don't benefit from reminders embedded in a process or calendar to help them stay on track.

Remember, our brains are seeking comfort. If employees have not yet fully adopted a new behavior, if it still feels uncomfortable and awkward, they are more likely to slip back into old patterns. Reminders are key to helping an individual change current, well-established brain patterns into the new brain patterns that are necessary for meeting a new goal. Reminders can take myriad forms, including meetings, calendar appointments, and even step-by-step processes posted around the workplace. The scale and urgency of the desired change should influence the types of reminders a manager chooses to help the team shift behaviors in time to ensure success.

Dr. Jane Nelson's *Positive Discipline* offers excellent information and advice about developing effective and efficient habits. The book is aimed at parents trying to guide toddlers into new habits, such as a morning routine. Before you throw up your hands in exasperation, keep this in mind: Toddlers are working with the same hardware as your employees—the wonderfully complex, sometimes frustratingly stubborn human brain.

So, what does Dr. Nelsen recommend to help toddlers adopt new habits and stay focused? A colorful poster with the routine spelled out step by step, posted in a conspicuous place. Does this sound like a well-documented process, easily available to employees who need some help remembering exactly how to approach a new way of working? Aside from gold stars and construction paper, it's almost exactly the same thing.[41]

Let's suppose you would like your vice president of business development to begin a new focus on profit per customer. The two of you agree that she will pull this information monthly and make recommendations based on the data obtained.

If she has never gathered this information or put it to use in the past, the habit is not yet formed and the behavior is not yet comfortable. As her manager, it's up to you to schedule a monthly discussion about the data, which will serve as a reminder for her to pull the information and allow you to coach her on using it.

As leaders, both of us encouraged our employees to use calendar appointments as reminders for new habits. In this case, as managers, we would encourage the vice president of business development to set a calendar reminder to pull the profit-per-customer information two or three days prior to our monthly meetings. We would then support her by ensuring she is comfortable with the process of extracting the data, and possibly offer her a step-by-step guide.

Even a seemingly simple process can fall by the wayside over the course of a month. As described in *Positive Discipline*, a simple step-by-step process can be an efficiency booster while a habit is being formed.

Again, reminders can take many forms—a meeting, a calendar appointment, a posted set of instructions. It's important to work with employees to understand how they will feel most supported and what they need to adopt a new habit as quickly as possible.

Step 4: Again and Again and... Yep, Again

If a team leader has something that's important enough to communicate, he or she should take the time to communicate it in the way that individuals are most likely to really hear and retain it. So many leaders find the one-off email or the single killer speech to be the defining cornerstone of their communication plan. This is not conducive to learning, adoption, or high performance.

Find ways to repeat the same information using different methods. As consultants, we often follow up an in-person session with a series of phone calls, which have additional information and structured discussion. You can host an internal webinar or record a webinar for team members to watch when it's most convenient for them.

One method that can increase engagement and spread ideas quickly is a one-time book club, essentially a series of guided discussions for a single book. While an ongoing book club can be challenging to maintain, a group of team members who are willing to volunteer their time to increase their expertise in innovation, efficiency, data, or even marketing will approach guided discussions with enthusiasm and a willingness to champion the message. We have implemented this successfully at a number of companies and watched as influencers gained the expertise to become true champions.

As the book club comes to a close, at least one or two meetings should be devoted to group discussion and planning around applying one or two key concepts from the book to the organization.

Finally, the international consulting firm McKinsey promotes an excellent approach to learning: the field-and-forum approach. This approach takes into account that adult learning requires the brain to actually create new neural pathways, which takes time and application. Therefore, training or new processes are not shared with employees in one large block. Instead, leaders or trainers deliver in-person learning and communication modules (the forum), which are followed by fieldwork assignments (the field). Each module builds on the previous one, with time in between for application and practice. This approach to learning and development suits how the brain absorbs and applies information much better than intensive data dumps do.

Remember, if you as a team leader are sick of talking about the new strategy, your team is probably just starting to feel really comfortable with it. As the team leader, it is your responsibility to share information in a way that makes it as easy as possible for team members to absorb.

Armed with a solid foundation, a set of clear strategic goals, and a highly engaging communication plan, your organization's performance improvement effort is off to a very strong start.

Checklist for Strategic Communication

- Before you hit send for an email, make sure you have either already communicated or have planned a future date for communicating the message in-person or via webinar.

- Kickoffs for new strategic plans or other change efforts should be scaled according to the level of organizational impact of the new plan and the geography of the team.

- Prepare other team leaders to be ready for coaching and truckloads of feedback.

- Prior to communicating the strategy, have a plan in place for creating mechanisms and reminders that will support the new behaviors necessary for team success.

- Communicate in a myriad of ways on a myriad of dates. Schedule forums, group phone calls, webinars, office hours, and, yes, emails. Just make sure your delivery of information is coordinated and consistent.

Case Study: Contra Costa Federal Credit Union

Contra Costa Federal Credit Union (CCFCU) was founded in 1949 with just thirty-four members. For over fifty years it has steadfastly served the public employees of Contra Costa County, California, growing to over twenty-seven-thousand members and five branches. The credit union has a history of focusing on excellent customer service. Over the decades it had settled comfortably into its long-established practices and performance.

Its financials were steady, and its employees were happy with the status quo.

Then in 2008, the Great Recession swept through the financial industry like a pandemic. The revenue from interest on loans that many banks and credit unions relied on was drastically reduced as interest rates for borrowers were driven lower and lower. Banks and credit unions were only as strong as the loans on their books and only as agile as their workforce. If either proved weak, failure was usually the result—meaning shutting the doors or being absorbed by a larger, stronger financial entity.

CCFCU had made decades of prudent loans to members, meaning the loan principal was paid back in full and on time. The threat to CCFCU lay in the quickly diminishing interest revenue. CEO David Green began to question how the credit union would survive the recession and continue to operate in the future. Interest was the main source of revenue and profit for the credit union, and as market rates were squeezed, profits plummeted. The business model of relying primarily on interest revenue quickly became unsustainable.

Green recognized a dangerous downward trend in the financials and called a meeting with the board of directors. He began the meeting by laying out a dire picture of the credit union's current path and told the board, "If we don't change something, we won't exist. We can't do what we did forty years ago." If the credit union was to survive the recession intact and independent, it had to quickly identify the right changes to improve performance.

Green's presentation to the board built a strong sense of urgency. The board agreed with him that the organization had to change or face closure. It was time to discuss a plan for reversing the dangerous financial trend. Green presented four potential options:

- Riskier loans—The credit union could decide to lower its standards for loan qualifications and charge higher interest rates for the riskier loan portfolio. This option carried the risk of greater loan defaults and the higher costs of administration associated with them.

- Riskier investments—Shrinking profits could be invested into riskier securities with potentially greater reward. Of course, this option came with the potential for a greater loss.

- Higher fees—Following in the footsteps of other major banking institutions, the credit union could choose to increase fees on its current service offerings, such as checking accounts. This proposal conflicted with the norms and culture of the credit union and was considered highly undesirable.

- Increased loan volume and services per member—Many members of the credit union used services such as debit cards, credit cards, and checking accounts from other banks. Members also often sought loans from other financial institutions first. By offering all these services through CCFCU, they would be able to collect low fees for each service while offering greater convenience to members.

The four options presented both new revenue opportunities and potential values conflicts for the credit union. Each option had to be evaluated with several criteria in mind: the need for increased revenue, member interests, a history of conservative lending, and a culture that valued strong relationships over strong sales tactics.

Both Green and the board overwhelmingly supported the fourth option. Because members of a credit union are also beneficiaries of its profits through dividends, Green and the board were wary of increasing the risk of either the loan or investment portfolio. Low fees had historically been a major differentiator between CCFCU and larger banks—a competitive advantage no one wanted to lose.

By increasing the number of services available to members but keeping fees traditionally low, CCFCU could be financially sustainable while offering an even more robust array of services for members. "We needed to sell our other products to make the members feel engaged and comfortable to come to us for a loan in the future," remarked Green. The change vision now driving performance improvement at CCFCU was that of a transformation from an order-taking reactive environment to a high-touch, high-service sales culture.

The problem was, the current CCFCU team didn't have what it took to create the culture they needed. Green began to formulate a plan that would eventually transform CCFCU's performance and reverse the negative trend.

First, Green knew that the entire CCFCU team needed a clear objective. They needed line of sight, a specific metric that every employee could get behind. Taking a page from Jim Collins' *Good to Great*, Green defined a "Big, Hairy, Audacious Goal"—to sell 150,000 products and services to members. Progress toward this goal would serve as the metric for company performance. Green also identified two additional transformational objectives: a short-term goal of two services per member and a long-term goal of three services per member. CCFCU had already begun tracking these numbers and had a head start of 50,000 products and services sold. Green decided to forego a deadline for the goals: "Having an unreasonable end date would stress out the staff, so I kept it open-ended and promised a big party when we hit our goal."

One major challenge sat squarely between the CCFCU team and achievement of their goals: Selling another 100,000 services and products to members required comfort with, well, sales. Comfort with sales was in scant supply among CCFCU team members. As Green explained, "My biggest challenge was to figure out how to motivate the staff without quotas and incentives. The new staff with the mega-bank experience left because they did not like the high-pressure sales culture, and the newbies with little experience but the capability did not have the formal training. I came up with a different approach. I determined team goals in which we would all participate."

Green realized he needed to create a sales culture without scaring away high-performing employees or CCFCU members. He recognized that not every team member had the tools or skills to successfully contribute to the goals that would keep the credit union financially stable. Think back to the definition of line of sight: an individual's clear understanding of the specific objectives and behaviors that contribute to overall company success. Green acted quickly to ensure that the objectives and behaviors were clear and accountable.

With clear metrics outlined, Green moved to enhance line of sight and increase comfort with sales behaviors. The three tactics Green credits most with a total shift in company culture and achieving CCFCU's performance improvement are the following:

1. Providing monthly metric feedback

A goal of 100,000 products and services can seem overwhelming as a total. To break the goal into motivating, actionable numbers, Green identified three key metrics to report monthly to team members:

- a running total of products and services sold to show progress toward the main goal

- a monthly total of products and services sold, which allowed the team members to identify trends and work to increase sales month over month

- average number of services per member

Average number of services per member became a driver of change, since it forced team members to consider important services members may have been missing out on. Team members worked to move this number from one to two in the short term, then to three in the long term. Each of these metrics created a strong link for team members between their actions and long-term company success.

2. Hiring a sales coach

Green regularly asked his staff, "What do you need to make this goal?" The most common response was that they were uncomfortable starting a conversation with members about additional services. Green realized that his team needed coaching.

In terms of line of sight, team members didn't always know the specific actions or behaviors that would support goal success. Green decided to bring in outside help so the team could learn the best actions and behaviors for meeting the company goal. By bringing in a professional sales coach, Green sent a message to the team that "we all could use some support in this area; let's learn together."

Rather than reinvent the wheel, the team members learned tried-and-true ways to build stronger connections with members and ensure that CCFCU was meeting all of its financial needs.

3. Instituting buddy meetings

"The whole thing could have failed without the buddy meetings," Green declared. He recognized that team members would be most comfortable learning about CCFCU services from other team members over time. A loan officer might not know every detail of the banking services offered, and a member services representative might not know the current rates offered for a thirty-year mortgage. But together, they could learn more about each other's specialties and have specific team members to refer customers to for more information.

Buddy meetings are held once a month at all the credit union branches. The meetings bring most of the team members together to discuss member experiences and cross-selling best practices. "We ask each person to tell us something good or bad that has come up in the past month with regards to cross-selling," Green elaborated.

The buddy meetings have created a safe space to sharpen new skills and support a strong culture of accountability in which individuals are regularly expected to share their efforts to achieve the overall company goal.

Growing Success

CCFCU's goal of selling 100,000 new products and services will take time to achieve, but the average rate of services and products sold monthly is currently over 250 and increases every month. In just two years, CCFCU managed to increase the average services per member from 1.75 to 2.

As members have increased the number of services they use at the credit union, revenues have risen. The CCFCU team has reversed the negative revenue trend and is now working toward increasing profits and dividends to members.

Green's biggest win? A total team performance improvement that has been sustained for over two years with continually increasing momentum. The culture has shifted completely from reactive order taking to proactive matching of members with services and products. Every aspect of CCFCU is now aligned with this level of performance, including metrics, hiring, compensation, and coaching.

Accountability

Green knew from the get-go that he had to model both accountability and discipline in order for this cultural shift and performance improvement to take hold: "I had seen change attempted before where the discipline was lacking. After three months everyone looked around and asked, 'What happened to it?' Now that our survival depends on it, there's no letting up."

From the beginning, Green made it crystal clear that the credit union would go out of business unless every team member adopted specific behaviors that increased service and product revenue.

Green also clearly communicated the positive consequences of supporting the change effort and the negative consequences of refusing or resisting it. He worked closely with management to promote and reward those within the organization who modeled the new behaviors and contributed to goal success. Those who were unwilling to change either left of their own accord, received coaching to work toward success, or, in some cases, were demoted.

CCFCU's combination of buddy meetings and monthly metrics reporting established a clear line of sight. The metrics and meetings offered constant feedback and regular opportunities to internalize the connections between individual behaviors and company success. If either the buddy meetings or the metrics reporting had faded away or fizzled out, the performance improvement would have followed suit.

Creating a culture of accountability requires checking in on goal progress consistently and using the information gathered to drive any needed calibrations in behavior. It's in coming together to discuss both metrics and experiences that individuals recognize the significance of their contributions and continued effort.

Green described coaching as paramount to changing team member behaviors: "We made sure we clearly outlined the behaviors we needed. If managers witnessed an action that could be improved, they coached immediately. It's important to get to the team and give the feedback immediately." CCFCU leadership also recognized that coaching is constant calibration. Green explains that to achieve this constant calibration, the credit union "set up a system that monitors the success rate of our selling and forces staff to summarize their conversations with members and what, if any, the next step is to get the member to buy a product or service."

Green decided early on to lead by example by being completely open to giving and receiving feedback. He admitted that sales had never been his strong suit and he had quite a bit to learn. Green's openness and discipline were exactly the leadership traits needed for a long-term performance improvement. Today he recognizes that even as the team continues to improve, the effort will continue to require unyielding support from CCFCU leadership: "What I can do is connect sales with future financial success and remind the staff constantly our successes as a team will have a positive outcome on the future of our credit union."

Part IV

Individual Performance

Chapter 10

What Annual Performance Review?

Imagine yourself sitting down with two CEOs. One leads a top-performing graphic design firm that's growing by double digits each year. The other heads up a stagnating office supply chain that has contracted in size the last three years running and is currently in a downward spiral of employee performance. These two CEOs do have at least one thing in common. If we were to ask both of them how last year's annual performance reviews went, they would both respond, "What annual performance reviews?"

On a spectrum that spans from no performance management on one end to the most progressive, evidence-based employee development system on the other, the annual performance review sits squarely in the middle. Although this practice is stubbornly embedded in American management culture, study after study shows that at best, it is minimally effective, and at worst, downright detrimental to performance. In their 2011 article "Why Is Performance Management Broken?" Pulakos and O'Leary argue that "communicating what employees are expected to do, providing feedback, and helping employees contribute the most they can are essential behaviors managers must engage in to accomplish work through others. Done effectively, performance management communicates what's important to the organization, drives employees to achieve results, and implements the organization's strategy. Done poorly, performance management not only fails to achieve these benefits but can also undermine employee confidence and damage relationships. The extremely large number of unsuccessful attempts to improve performance management speaks volumes about its inherent difficulties."[42]

Each of the behaviors described by Pulakos and O'Leary are part of a continual process throughout the year, not aspects of a once-per-year exercise. It's important to distinguish that an annual performance review is *not* synonymous with performance management.

Pulakos and O'Leary describe a performance management approach that supports performance improvement precisely as we have prescribed in the previous two sections. Communicating goals clearly, motivating employees to reach their potential, and creating a strong line-of sight-strategy are now familiar concepts. These concepts run through almost every single piece of team-performance literature for a reason: They work.

This book shows you how to take an entire organization and the teams within it to the next level of performance, but nothing gives you more power to improve overall performance than fostering the performance of each individual team member.

A Winning Team Requires Successful Individuals

Developing the performance of individuals is the single most powerful way to increase long-term, sustainable growth. And the best way to develop individual performance is through a performance management system that brings focus to career successes and pinpoints areas of low performance.

Let's pause for a moment to further define the difference between performance management and annual performance review. Many of today's leaders use these terms interchangeably. Rest assured that by the end of this chapter, you will never be confused with one of those leaders.

Performance management is a system of practices and policies that create predictable rewards and consequences for effort, results, and for exemplifying the values of an organization.

The annual performance review is one of many practices from which to choose when designing the right performance management system for an organization or team. Examples of other performance management practices include regular one-on-one check-ins, individual development plans, and performance improvement plans.

The Myth of the Annual Performance Review

In our experience, the annual performance review is one of the most dreaded practices in organizations today, bested only by annual budgeting and any trust-building exercise involving blindfolds. On its face, the performance review seems like a harmless, if not empowering, feedback conduit. What employees wouldn't want performance feedback that points out their strengths and guides them toward greatness? If the annual performance review actually delivered this, it would be our number-one prescription for improving team and individual performance. But the annual performance review isn't even among our top ten recommendations, because it so rarely lives up to what it's purported, or even intended, to be.

More often than not, the annual performance review involves an employee who brings a list of accomplishments and development aspirations to a conversation with a manager who is biologically programmed to remember the most recent few months of results, which he or she inaccurately extrapolates into a long-term trend. Combine this with the inescapable feeling of being judged (which in some cases is not a feeling, but in fact a ranking process that brings with it all the exciting baggage of being picked for a team in fourth grade), and it's very easy to understand why employees and managers alike struggle to get out the pom-poms for annual review season.

Okay, so performance reviews are hard, but done right they are still valuable, aren't they? Josh Bersin, talent management expert and founder of Bersin by Deloitte, has been tracking the corporate value of performance management, and in particular annual performance appraisals, since 2006. Bersin wrote recently that his firm's latest data show that "fewer than 30% of all organizations feel their existing process drives any level of performance or engagement at all (rather it simply helps evaluate people for compensation and promotion)."[43]

At this point, you may find yourself feeling as we did when we first dug into the research on annual performance reviews and discovered their less-than-stellar qualities: Resistant. Frustrated. Disbelieving. After all, would the vast majority of firms engage in a practice that offers no value? It would be irrational, against their best interest, and therefore thrown out of the playbook decades ago… right?

Let's take a moment to examine the most common reasons we hear for engaging in annual performance reviews:

1. All employees deserve to get feedback on their performance.

2. It's important to take stock of the past year and determine whether or not goals were accomplished.

3. There isn't much time day to day to discuss employee development; the annual performance review ensures that managers have a development plan in place for team members.

4. We need a method of determining who receives a bonus or a promotion.

Is any one of these a bad reason to engage in an annual performance review? Not in the least. The problem lies with the expectation that the annual performance review will actually *meet* all of these needs in a tightly wrapped, one- or two-meeting package that keeps the crying and defensive outbursts to a minimum.

The annual performance review is the New Year's resolution of performance management. It's time to improve! It's time to give feedback! It's time to *inspire!* By the month after the performance review, most people have forgotten all about it, and their basal ganglia have taken them right back to that comfortable status quo—until eleven months later, when it's time for another round of inspiring developmental feedback! Based on what you now know about behavioral change, does this sound like a recipe for continuous improvement?

Adopting a New Performance Management Mindset

Let's take a closer look at the reasons cited above for retaining this highly anticipated annual exercise.

1. All employees deserve to get feedback on their performance.

We could not agree more. Our research and experience lead us to believe that timely, specific, and fair feedback is the key to unlocking human performance potential. If an individual's work habits in May foreshadow a complete train wreck in terms of meeting annual goals, when is the best time to offer feedback? If you observed the actions of millions of managers, you would think the correct answer is "at the end of the year." We know you know that giving feedback six months late is a preposterous approach to high performance.

Sit down somewhere comfortable and prepare yourself. We are now going to give your brain the exact ammunition it needs to once and forever shed the paradigm of relying on the annual performance review for delivering feedback. In 2002 the Corporate Executive Board, a member-based advisory committee that boasts 90 percent of the Fortune 500 as clients, embarked on a quantitative analysis of performance management best practices. Here is what they uncovered:

Not only does [fair and accurate feedback] fall within the list of A-level performance strategies, **but it is also the single most important driver of performance across all 106 factors examined in this study**...

In fact, employees who receive fair and accurate feedback from their managers perform nearly 40 percent better than do employees who do not feel that the feedback they receive is fair or accurate. **Moreover, it is notable that the single largest performance driver is related to informal, rather than formal feedback** and is conducted at the manager level rather than the organizational level.[44]

Take special note (we bolded the important parts just so you can go back and read them again!): Fair and accurate *informal* feedback is not only the strongest driver of performance, it came out ahead of 106 other performance drivers. So, if fair, accurate, and informal feedback is *the* key to increased performance, how does the annual review process support this pivotal practice? Well, sorry to burst your performance management bubble, but it doesn't. At least not to the significant extent most managers think it does.

If you are the leader of a team within an organization that is holding onto the annual performance review as a sacred ritual, fret not. There are great leaders who manage to take this potentially rote activity and turn it into a truly positive and motivating experience for their teams. Further ahead in the chapter we'll outline exactly how they do this.

2. It's important to take stock of the past year and determine whether or not goals were accomplished.

Fair, accurate, and informal feedback must be timely in order to be effective. "Timely" as in once every few *days*—not once a *year.* Remember our discussion about the danger of reviewing your revenue and profit numbers at the end of year? If your only scheduled review occurs at the end of the year, are you in any position to improve that year's performance? Not in the least. That entire year passed you by, and any opportunity to improve those numbers went with it. The performance of your team members is no different. Wait until December to give them feedback on their productivity or lack of time management, and your ability to help them deliver twelve months of stronger performance has disappeared.

Steering a team to success requires constant small changes in navigation. These small changes effectively act as tiny continuous doses of learning and development in the form of feedback. This feedback sets the stage for better and more informed decisions on a daily basis.

Amy Edmonsdson, Richard Bohmer, and Gary Pisano studied "how surgical teams at sixteen major medical centers implemented a difficult new procedure for performing cardiac surgery."[45] They published their findings in the *Harvard Business Review*, reporting that a constant flow of information led to successful learning and better procedural outcomes—which may create a new imperative to engage in a somewhat awkward conversation about performance management with any cardiac surgeon you may one day meet in the operating room. Edmonson, Bohmer, and Pisano reported that, "[cardiac] teams whose members felt comfortable making suggestions, trying things that might not work, pointing out potential problems, and admitting mistakes were more successful in learning the new procedure. By contrast, when people felt uneasy acting this way, the learning process was stifled."[46]

Every team has its different measurements of success. If a cardiac team is not meeting its goals, people die. Waiting until the end of the year to give feedback on so-so surgical performance isn't an option. With the cardiac team, just as with your team, the ability to learn from a steady flow of measurement and informal feedback is the precise skill needed to increase performance. What happens if you drastically reduce the frequency of that feedback, giving it only once a year?

The brain unfortunately can hold only so much information at one time. Giving it a year's worth of feedback one day per year is like watering your lawn for twenty-four hours at the beginning of summer and hoping that one drenching will see it through the following hot months. Your lawn can absorb only so much water at once; the rest flows down the sidewalk.

The same is true with a deluge of feedback at the end of the year. The brain is an astonishing machine, capable of storing massive amounts of information. However, it has to process and sort all the new information, which it can do only in small quantities, not in one large upload.

A year-end wrap up is actually an incredibly effective way to recap and recount a year's worth of feedback. Imagine if, instead of cramming fifty-two weeks' worth of observations onto one page of ratings, you sat with a team member and reviewed accomplishments, lessons learned, and next year's development opportunities—again. The best managers have been engaged in this conversation throughout the entire year, formally and informally. The annual performance review then becomes a milestone, a miniature strategic retreat for individual performance. The anxiety and frustration are gone because there are no surprises and no fear of judgment.

In summary, it *is* important to take stock at the end of the year and review whether or not goals were accomplished. But it's much *more* important to offer informal feedback on a daily basis to ensure continuous learning, growth, and performance improvement.

3. There isn't much time day to day to discuss employee development; the annual performance review ensures that managers have a development plan in place for team members.

Hey, we get it. One client we worked with came back from a week's vacation to nearly a thousand emails. While it's possible that this manager needs a stronger spam filter, it's more likely that he—and most of us—have more to accomplish in one day than hours to do it in.

Briefly, let's go back to the concept of developing new habits over a period of time discussed at the beginning of the book. The benefit of the tactics we recommend is that they increase the efficiency, motivation, and effectiveness of each individual on your team. The challenge is to find the right amount of ongoing measurement, checking-in, and feedback to elicit an outcome with greater returns than your time investment.

The annual performance review is an excellent opportunity to review an employee's development plan and discuss which skills and abilities the employee should continue to strengthen. The annual performance review is not, however, a reliable tool for development if it serves as the only time a manager and employee discuss development goals. Setting one goal at the beginning of a new year is easily comparable with another habit—New Year's resolutions. Dr. John Norcross at the University of Scranton studied New Year's resolution success and found that of the people he studied, only 19 percent had kept their resolution two years later.[47]

Remember, in order to develop new skills or improve current ones, we have to learn new habits and new ways of behaving. In order to accomplish behavioral change, our brains literally need to be rewired. New Year's resolutions often fail because there are no long-term mechanisms in place to support the rewiring needed for new habits. Given that new behaviors and new skills require action, practice, and timely feedback in order to be embedded into our brains, is relying on the annual performance review for behavioral change a smart bet from a neurological standpoint? It's probably about as effective as everyone in the office making New Year's resolutions.

As with feedback, some managers make the best of an organization-wide annual review process by partnering with employees to set new development goals, then taking the next crucial step to outline a plan to ensure new habits, skill development, and feedback. This approach to development, with mechanisms for learning and coaching, is exactly what's needed to support the brain in making the connections for long-term behavioral change.

One statistic supported this learning and development approach that has shaped how we approach performance management with clients. Frankly, this statistic rocked our management foundations to the core. We knew that there are many approaches to increasing individual performance and that are all needed at some level to produce consistently high performance. What we never imagined was that, according to the Corporate Leadership Council, informal feedback that is perceived as fair and accurate has the potential to *change individual performance by 39 percent.*[48]

Pulakos and O'Leary outlined similar findings in their meta research, asserting that "[research] specifically highlights the importance of continuous feedback to help employees make real-time alterations in their behavior, enabling them to perform their work more efficiently and effectively."[49]

Imagine the power of setting development goals and, instead of placing bets that your team members will find the time and ability to rewire their brains entirely on their own, you support them in this effort with continuous, fair, and accurate informal feedback. You are now giving them the tools and information they need to potentially improve their performance by 39 percent.

4. We need a method of determining who receives a bonus or a promotion.

In any organization, positions and resources for team members are finite, so determining how to distribute them becomes a complex process. We would like to point out that this process is different for every organization based on culture, objectives, and talent pool. We can't cover every aspect of compensation and career planning because both topics could fill their own books (and have—there are dozens available).

Instead, we want to focus on the two aspects of performance management that ensure you are able to apply the data to career and compensation planning no matter which process you use for either. *Objective data* and *performance journaling* are two facets of performance management that enable team leaders to draw clear distinctions among team members and then make evidence-based decisions about how best to distribute the finite positions and resources available. It's important to understand why you need these two facets of performance management when you already have a pretty powerful tool—your brain—at your disposal. After all, you observe your team members on a daily basis. Wouldn't you remember their performance and thus have a common-sense understanding of who deserves a bonus or promotion for work completed during the past year?

We need to add one more uncomfortable truth to our growing list of reasons not to rely on the annual performance review: Unfortunately, your brain is a fairly *unreliable* tool when it comes to remembering someone's long-term performance objectively. *Recency bias* is a psychological phenomenon that describes the very real twist our brains give to our memories. In order to prevent an information overload, our brains focus on the most recent events (a few weeks to a few months) as representative of long-term trends. The problem with this efficient neurological process is that, as you know, one month's worth of observations may not be at all representative of the whole year's performance.

Have you ever come down with pneumonia, encountered trouble selling a home, or had one of your perfect children hit her teenage years? Every one of these phenomena could create distraction or temporary absenteeism for even the highest performer. If any one of these happens to occur in the two months prior to the annual performance review, even the most empathetic leaders may find their perspective on a year's worth of performance colored by frustration over missed deadlines or unanswered emails.

I've spoken with many leaders who have decreased planned salary increases or called potential promotions into question over "recent behavior." Most often, these same leaders have not taken even the first step toward finding out from the employee what might be causing a sudden spike in absences or stress. Making rash decisions about salary and career growth based on unexplored dips in behavior is a surefire way to send high performers searching for a new team that *will* value their long-term contributions.

As a high-performing team leader, you can counter your brain's tendency to translate recent events into long-term trends by ensuring that you are taking objective measurements of performance throughout the year. As recommended in the previous section, you should work toward taking appropriately frequent measurements of goals and key performance indicators for the organization, team, and individual. Some measurements will be quantitative, some qualitative, but most should be measured at a higher frequency than once a year. The most common frequency is once a month.

Creating an annual measurement plan for your individual team members triggers you to collect objective samples of data all year round, providing you with the information necessary to track long-term performance trends.

So, you're feeling all smug with your balanced scorecard, monthly measurements, and management prowess. But wait, what exactly are you going to do with all these data? This is where you call upon the wonderful habit of performance journaling.

Not unlike your youthful journals chronicling first crushes and getting a driver's license, a performance journal creates a longitudinal outline of milestones and performance, with entries at regular intervals. In other words, about once a month or so, you make an entry listing the goal measurements and notes relevant to a particular team member's performance.

A performance journal can be as simple as a Word document maintained for a year with monthly bulleted entries or as sophisticated as a cloud performance management system, which costs hundreds of thousands of dollars. The level of sophistication depends on the size and complexity of your organization.

If you are looking for a system to ensure that you are consistently taking a performance temperature for future salary increases or promotions, then measuring objective data and keeping a performance journal is the simplest, most elegant solution. If you work in an organization that requires annual performance reviews, you now have a quantitative and qualitative diary of real-time measurement and feedback, enabling you to bypass our friend recency bias in favor of an inspirational year-end capstone conversation.

We also recommend engaging in salary and promotion conversations separate from annual performance review development conversations. Understandably, focus on salary and promotions can and will overwhelm an employee's ability to absorb the highly valuable discussion about everything else.

Think back to the beginning of this chapter when we invited you to envision yourself sitting in front of two CEOs, one high performing and the other stagnant, but both surprised when you asked them about their annual performance review system. How is it possible that both the stagnant CEO and the skyrocketing CEO are forgoing performance reviews? The CEO with the struggling organization gives no priority to measuring or improving performance, which has tipped his organization into a downward spiral from which there may be no escape. With no mechanism to stop it, bad performance will only breed more bad performance.

The other CEO, with a rapidly growing bottom line and an even faster growing list of talent waiting to join the team, never implemented performance reviews because she knew there were more efficient ways to give feedback, take stock of goal progress, develop employees, and distribute resources than the dreaded annual judgment.

While these two CEOs are fictional, they represent real-world executives we have partnered with. Unfortunately, in more than one case like the first one, the companies did eventually fold, unable to steer performance in any meaningful way.

Some of today's most progressive large companies, including Netflix, Adobe, Juniper, and Gap, Inc., are all ditching annual performance reviews in favor of a performance management system that delivers a true novelty: increased performance and happier employees.

Without the Review, How Do We Manage?

Letting go of any habit, especially one so treasured as the annual review, can be scary. What if accountability goes with it? What if my team feels either abandoned or micromanaged if I approach management in a different way?

Rest assured that a mountain of evidence backs your decision to apply new methods to development and performance improvement. When you feel tempted to run back to the annual performance review with open arms, remember the following:

- *Informal* feedback is the driving force behind performance improvement.

- Objective data gathered continuously in regular intervals provides a more accurate basis for feedback than a written summary of the past three months of observations.

- Frequent performance journaling helps ensure feedback is timely, fair, and accurate.

- The brain is not capable of hearing, processing, and putting into action a year's worth of feedback at once.

- You can't leave your team's performance to chance.

Letting go of a stalwart process such as the annual performance review isn't easy. It takes courage to take a new, innovative approach to something that often feels sacred to many employees. But we have often observed that clients who pilot a new performance management system for two or three months find that teams embrace the new approach and are genuinely interested in moving toward a more valuable process. Often a pilot is an easy way to minimize the sense of risk associated with something new.

Any pilot includes objectives, a plan, a timeframe, and some form of evaluation. When employees understand that their opinions will be heard at the end of a pilot run, they often feel more comfortable trying out something new. In our experience, team members find more frequent feedback incredibly engaging, and they aren't the least bit interested in going back.

Five Easy Ways to Increase Individual Success

1. Schedule standing, monthly, one-on-one check-ins.

Or heck, go crazy and have biweekly check-ins. The frequency will depend on the size of your team, the complexity of your work, and your proximity to your team members.

As leaders and consultants, we have even chosen to hold weekly check-ins with our direct reports, a habit that many of our most successful clients have adopted.

Once you have become an accountability Ninja, supporting your team members in performance and development, you might find that the frequency of your check-ins decreases to monthly. This is completely fine.

Whether you start at weekly and go to monthly, or start at biweekly and find that weekly suits you best, this practice is all about finding the right frequency for informal feedback, goal review, and development dialogue.

2. Prepare a schedule for measuring progress on goals.

Building off the schedule you've developed for measuring KPIs, bring measurement down to an individual level. The information you gather will fuel your check-ins and ensure you are able to make data-driven decisions in real time to coach team members to success.

Goal measurements don't have to take place as frequently as your check-ins, but you should establish a regular rhythm of reviewing the data with your team members one on one. Even if you are having biweekly check-ins, a monthly goal review can still be very effective.

3. Create a basic agenda for the check-ins.

Vistage chairman Peter Michaels is an accountability partner and coach for CEOs. He meets with them monthly to check in on goals, commitments, and emotional health. (CEOs need accountability, too!) He begins every check-in with the same question: "What is the most important thing we should be talking about today?"

We have used this simple question for years and have found it to be invaluable. It allows team members to present to you what is uppermost in their minds. Because our minds are wired to focus on the negative, it's most likely a stressor or obstacle that gets presented. This empowers you as a leader to coach your direct report in overcoming stressors and removing obstacles to success. Over time, your team members become more and more adept at overcoming challenges on their own in the moment.

Whether the most important thing your team member shares is negative or positive, it is most likely something you didn't expect and typically is something you wouldn't have heard about until it was too late to fix or celebrate. Because you made the choice to set aside one-on-one time for your team member, you will often be rewarded with the information you need to lead your team to a successful year.

4. Maintain a performance journal.

Whether it's a running Word document, an Excel workbook with a worksheet for every month, or a sophisticated, cloud-based performance management platform, find a way to keep a running narrative of each team member's successes and opportunities for development.

A financial services client we work with created a goal-tracking spreadsheet that requires the manager and employee to measure goal-based results each month and enter them on the spreadsheet to track progress throughout the year. An additional worksheet is devoted to the monthly performance and development narrative.

We partnered with this particular client for almost fifteen months, and together we outlined their foundation and balanced scorecard; we then customized a performance management system that allowed their managers to easily manage individual performance, hold team members accountable, and continually offer informal feedback. The lesson here is that you can choose performance journaling as the first tool you implement from this book, but the practice becomes much more meaningful and motivational if it's tied to the purpose, values, and key performance indicators that underpin the success of your organization.

5. Adopt a habit of giving informal feedback

Doling out timely, accurate, and fair feedback on a daily basis doesn't come naturally to most. As a leader, however, it needs to become as natural to you as sleeping and eating. This kind of feedback should roll off your tongue at least a couple of times during meetings and occur naturally when you pass a team member in the hallway. Pulakos and O'Leary offer these guidelines for providing continuous informal feedback: "Informal feedback is different in nature than formal feedback. First, it typically deals with a specific matter rather than a broader evaluation over time and multiple competencies. It can include strategizing what to do, deciding next steps, analyzing what went right or wrong, and/or discussing what to do differently next time. Formal feedback tends to be initiated, led, and controlled by the manager, whereas informal feedback relies more heavily on two-way accountability and interaction."[50]

As leaders, we started out far from this ideal. Not knowing the value of informal feedback, we starved our teams of feedback, thinking there just wasn't the time or that we'd get to it during the annual review. You are no longer ignorant of the power of your informal feedback, and now that you've read this chapter, you are never allowed to make those excuses again.

So, how did we go about adopting a habit of informal feedback? Two ways:

a. Scheduling it.

Seven years ago, if you had opened up our calendars, you would have seen entries on Mondays, Wednesdays, and Fridays reminding us to give two pieces of fair and accurate feedback. These reminders supported the discipline necessary to make feedback natural for us. The sheer excitement and increase in motivation from our teams within one week of beginning the practice of regular informal feedback kept us enthusiastic. We've been known to give positive performance feedback to complete strangers at stores and restaurants and have been amazed at how much people appreciate it.

b. Using if-then statements.

Dr. Jeremy Dean promotes this method of habit building in his *Making Habits, Breaking Habits: Why We Do Things, Why We Don't and How To Make Any Change Stick*. If-then statements create rules for your brain and support discipline when you're trying to adopt a new habit. Our if-then statements included, "if a team member brings a piece of work for us to discuss or review, then I will give accurate and fair feedback," and "if we are in a meeting where ideas are being shared, then I will give at least one piece of accurate and fair feedback."[51]

It's important to keep in mind that you should give more positive feedback than negative. Remember, our brains focus on the negative (pesky, survival-oriented hardware). As a leader, you need to balance this negative focus by working to offer five pieces of positive feedback for each constructive one. For some leaders, just working on a 1:1 ratio is a step in the right direction.

Start with a goal that both makes sense for you and stretches you. We often recommend a ratio of 3:1, or at the least 2:1, but taking some time to work up to the desired ratio will ensure that giving positive feedback feels more natural and therefore more sustainable for your leadership.

If you are the leader of an organization, you are now empowered to build an evidence-based performance management system that delivers performance results, rather than simply retroactive reviews. If you are a team leader within an organization that requires annual reviews, you now have a practical, easily applicable guide to putting the annual performance review to productive use as the capstone of a truly effective yearlong coaching practice.

Now that you are handing out high-fives in the hallway and engaging in regular feedback conversations with individuals on your team, journaling their performance, and ensuring that end-of-year results are entirely predictable, you are left with two significant questions:

- How do I develop my team members' skills and abilities beyond what they need for daily performance?

- How do I handle an individual who is not meeting performance expectations even with my support and continuous feedback?

These questions take us to the next level of exceptional performance management. Get ready to learn the answers in the next chapter.

Checklist for a Powerful Performance Management System

- Schedule regular check-ins with each individual on your team.

- Schedule the appropriate frequency for measurement for goals and KPIs.

- Create a performance journaling system.

- Outline your plan for adopting an informal feedback habit.

Chapter 11

The Art of Managing
Your Best and Worst Performers

The tools outlined in this chapter take you to the next level of exceptional leadership. The first tool will help you develop individual team members, and in particular will support the engagement and retention of top performers while preparing them for increased levels of responsibility. The second tool will empower you to expediently and compassionately coach low performers up to performance expectations or coach them out to opportunities that better fit their strengths and abilities.

The Individual Development Plan

If you served in the United States Military as Neal did, you will be very familiar with the Individual Development Plan, or IDP for short. An IDP outlines short- and long-term goals for an individual team member, then specifies the actions and resources necessary to achieve the goals.

A crucial distinction between IDP and performance goals is that IDP goals are not linked directly to the success of the team or organization, but rather are aimed at helping an individual acquire new skills and abilities or a deeper level of mastery in already acquired competencies.

As with a performance journal, an IDP can take many forms: a Word document, an Excel spreadsheet, or even a notebook in Evernote. Like performance journals, the format should be fairly consistent from one employee to another.

Many organizations wrap the annual development conversation into the annual performance review. Performance management expert Elaine Pulakos uses a case study to explain why you should steer clear of this approach:

Managers in [the] organization evaluate their employees and then meet to calibrate their ratings and make reward decisions. Managers then conduct review sessions with every employee to discuss the employee's performance, pay increase, and stock option grant.

Developmental feedback is supposed to be included in the meeting. However, the range of percentage increases and stock options is large, thereby allowing managers to link performance with rewards effectively. With so much at stake, the majority of the meeting typically focuses on justification by both parties, rather than on how the employee can develop.

The climate of the meeting is not conducive to giving and receiving feedback, and employees are reticent to discuss their development needs for fear this will negatively impact their rewards. Even in the strong performance-based culture of this organization, the decision-making aspect of performance is, by default, given more emphasis.[52]

"So," you might be thinking, "are you telling me that I need to maintain a performance journal, an individual development plan, and then have a separate process for salary increases?" We are, and it's not as time consuming as it might sound. The trick is to introduce these tools over the course of two or three years.

Recall that organizational measurement is a skill that requires intentional development and team effort over the course of a few years. With each passing year, the team is ready for more complex and more specific performance measures. Performance management is no different. Starting with monthly check-ins, then adding a performance journal, and eventually working up to an IDP is a process that should be approached patiently and in planned steps. It's typical that an organization would also approach a new performance management system as a one-to-three-year process.

Once regular check-ins and a performance journal are in place, most team leaders and all employees welcome the process of outlining an IDP. In many of today's industries and specialties, such as health care, human resources, software development, and engineering, it's an employee market. Your best performers always have the option to take their talent literally down the street. How much thought your team leaders put into IDPs can have a significant impact on employee retention.

Achieving High ROI through Employee IDPs

Employees who feel that their organization is invested in them are much more willing to invest their effort and loyalty into their organization. IDPs strike straight at the heart of your employees' intrinsic motivation, which ties them to the team for reasons beyond money. And the benefit of having employees formally outline goals that will make them continuously more effective in their roles is a great return on investment for spending a few hours developing an IDP.

We once worked with a construction client who actively sought veterans for project management roles. The problem was that this client didn't feel IDPs were a worthwhile effort. The veterans wouldn't stay with the company for more than six months or a year because their time in the military had accustomed them to expect formal development goals and accountability to them. Not only were the veterans disappointed that the organization wouldn't invest that effort in them over the long term, but they also felt the lack of IDPs reflected poorly on the management of the organization.

IDP Detailed How-To

So, what does an IDP entail exactly? Let's take a look at some common elements on IDP templates:

1. Employee's name, position, supervisor

2. Timeframe associated with the IDP

3. Knowledge and skill development goals

These goals should describe the specific skills or increase in knowledge that the employee hopes to acquire. If at the end of the IDP timeframe it's not clear how these goals are measured, then the goals are not specific enough.

4. Development assignments

These can be projects, cross-trainings, or even reading assignments that support the goal development.

5. Formal training and the training resource

Most organizations don't have the bandwidth for formal in-house training, so it's crucial that when formal training is expected, external resources and budgets are identified.

6. Development challenges

Dr. Gabriele Oettingen has devoted her career to studying the impacts of positive thinking on goal achievement—the *negative* impacts of positive thinking, that is. In study after study, Dr. Oettingen has shown that goals are much more likely to be achieved when individuals first envision achieving the goal, and then consider the obstacles that may prevent success.[53] This technique is called "mental contrasting," and it can be valuable for any type of goal-setting conversation.

How does it work? Mental contrasting either motivates the individual to overcome the obstacles and achieve the goal or empowers them to acknowledge that the goal isn't realistic.

As with any project plan, deadlines enable transparency of expectations and clear accountability. Don't finish an IDP without including expected completion dates of assignments and trainings.

The beginning of a calendar or fiscal year is an ideal time to create an IDP. Then, just as with performance goals, a monthly check-in is appropriate, but a bimonthly or quarterly check-in can work as well, depending on the types of assignments and frequency of training.

A small but renowned Australian software development firm, Atlassian, has experimented publicly with its performance management system. The firm assigns various topics to monthly one-on-one check-ins so that in the first month of the year, the topic is performance, in the second month it's development, and in the third it's what they call "love and loathe," which is just what it sounds like, except career focused.[54]

You have the power to create whatever will suit your team and motivate them to achieve their peak performance. Start out simple, add depth, and calibrate as necessary.

The Performance Improvement Plan

If you have a team member whose immediate resignation would incite relief and inappropriate high-fives, this next section is for you. The performance improvement plan, or PIP for short, is a powerful tool that leads to one of two outcomes: individual success or irrefutable evidence that the individual is not a fit for the role. Initiating the PIP requires a confident leader to start with, and the process of seeing the PIP through makes the leader even stronger.

In essence, the PIP is a sixty- or ninety-day plan that lays out the following in writing:

- A set of results and goals that define success in the position
- Descriptions of the actions needed to achieve the results
- The resources available to support skill development
- A check-in schedule to ensure accountability and coaching

We have been shocked by the number of ineffective team members who have been around for years, sometimes even *decades.* In our next section, we'll describe to you in fascinating, research-backed detail exactly how these low performers drag your team down and drive effective team members out. Right now, trust us that the team member whose resignation would elicit relief is making your top performers question their loyalty to the team *every single day.*

If your goal is to ensure that your team members feel valued and engaged, refusing to allow a low performer to disrupt their success is one of the clearest messages you can send. While it sounds cut and dry, the PIP is actually an extremely compassionate, supportive process. It often results in individuals choosing to leave the team once they realize they are not a good fit for it, which frees them to feel in control of their destiny and frees you from needing to terminate them.

If the low performers don't succeed or choose to leave, the PIP provides so much evidence of their skill mismatch that separation feels like the right thing for all parties. It's the only way the team and these individuals will find success in the long run.

It's Time for A PIP When...

Many organizations have their own progressive discipline procedures: first a verbal warning, then a written warning, then either a PIP or termination. The PIP fits in well with a progressive discipline plan since you will want to establish themes of missing goals, low skill levels, or interpersonal difficulties prior to embarking on a PIP. A PIP is not appropriate for someone who missed goals for the first quarter in three years or has had one embarrassing outburst in a meeting. It's for an unmistakable trend of either of these types of behaviors.

Here are some examples of situations in which we have worked with team leaders to implement a PIP:

- A previously successful insurance adjuster, with the organization for over five years, suddenly fell severely behind in his work and struggled for months to dig himself out from under a pile of claims.

- An accounts receivable manager's work suddenly lost accuracy, resulting in unacceptable work for a period of two months.

- A retail clerk was often found on social media sites instead of completing her substantial to-do list. More often than not, her to-do list was unfinished at the end of her day.

The PIPs for the first two situations uncovered the root causes of the poor performances and created a supportive foundation for catch up and regaining success. The third case is an excellent example of a PIP that resulted in the clear recognition that the employee's priorities did not match the organization's and she just wasn't a good fit for the position.

You'll know it's time for a PIP when you want to tell a team member that *something has to change.*

Preparing a PIP

As with many of the tools outlined in our book, a PIP can take many forms depending on your team and your organization. Doing a Google search for "performance improvement plan" and clicking on images will yield a number of prototypes to help you get started. It's possible your labor attorney has a preferred template as well. Otherwise, a simple Word document with the four main criteria is effective.

In preparing a PIP, you might feel that your actions are redundant. You've had many conversations and sent just as many emails that collectively contain all the information you've just outlined in the PIP. This is exactly how you should feel. None of the information in a PIP should be new. If your concerns had never been communicated to your employees before the

PIP, then they didn't have the information they needed to succeed, and it's important both for morale and litigation-risk reasons to give them the information and the opportunity to use it before you move to a PIP.

The language used in a PIP's introduction is vital to its efficacy, but it can also be risky if it's not reviewed by a labor attorney. Make sure you have the language reviewed before you implement the PIP. It's important to spell out in the introduction and conclusion that this tool is intended to support the individual's success, and if performance is not satisfactory at the end of the allotted period, actions up to and including termination may be taken. We are not attorneys, so make sure you work with one to craft this language for your organization.

When crafting the PIP, be as specific as possible. Recognize that the time you spend thoughtfully developing the PIP could unlock your employees' abilities to meet their goals. When you take it that seriously, the outcome is nearly always beneficial to the team one way or another. The PIP should include signature lines at the conclusion for the manager and employee to acknowledge that they have read and understood the document.

Delivering a PIP

If you have a human resources representative and/or employment attorney available to you, for development and legal reasons, you should work with one or both of them to do the following:

- Discuss the employee's trends and performance status to verify that a PIP is appropriate.
- Review the PIP document for clarity and objectivity.
- Determine whether or not having a third party present for the PIP delivery is appropriate.

Having the right third party present can enhance the seriousness of the situation. An HR representative or another manager who works tangentially with the employee can offer a different perspective and verify your observations and recommendations.

For legal reasons, it's never a bad idea to have someone else present to witness the conversation.

Schedule a time and place free from distraction to talk to the employee. Scheduling the meeting about a day in advance gives the employee time to adjust accordingly without too much time to stew and become increasingly anxious.

The meeting will consist of some introductory context setting and discussion of performance trends, followed by a review of the PIP document and discussion of next steps. Let the employee know that the document needs to be signed, but that he or she can propose edits or revisions to it before signing. Motivated employees may have valuable additions to the document; be sure to welcome these additions if they appropriately support the sought-after results.

Next, provide any resources you promised and schedule time for all the check-ins required by the PIP, ensuring that no excuses get in the way of reviewing progress.

Expect the Unexpected

Here are some of the most frequent and most important questions we receive about PIPs:

1. I'm afraid if I deliver this to my employee, she'll quit. How do I present this in a way that doesn't offend her?

We appreciate your sensitivity to her feelings. However, if receiving accurate and specific feedback on her performance, along with scheduled developmental support, is enough to make her pack her things, wish her the best and move on.

Remember, the point of a PIP is that *something has to change.* If at the conclusion of a skillfully delivered PIP the individual decides she isn't interested in that level of accountability, don't stand in the way of her decision to move on. This is a surprisingly common occurrence.

2. Do I maintain the PIP if his performance dramatically increases in the first couple of weeks?

You must see the entire PIP through to conclusion no matter how soon and how well the individual improves. Some individuals thrive with unsustainably intense levels of accountability and support from leadership, but their performance slips once the levels return to normal.

You will need to assess whether their results are due to a true change in actions and habits, or whether they just adjust their effort under pressure.

3. Do I maintain the PIP if it becomes clear the individual doesn't have the skills to succeed in the position?

You can mitigate litigation risk by seeing the entire PIP through to the end. However, if during the course of the PIP you discover something about the individual's skill level that makes clear that even with sixty or ninety days of development, the employee will not be able to achieve the desired results, you may choose to terminate him or her before the end of the PIP.

Language outlining your right to terminate should be included in the PIP document itself. You should always consult with an employment attorney before you terminate an employee, especially if that employee is on a PIP.

4. What should I do if the team member successfully finishes the PIP with results achieved, then performance dips again a month later?

This is the most complex situation, but it can be managed easily with planning. Some organizations, larger ones in particular, employ ninety-day, sixty-day, and thirty-day PIPs for just this scenario. A low-performing employee starts on a ninety-day PIP. If poor performance recurs, begin a sixty-day PIP and then, if necessary, a thirty-day PIP. If the employee cannot maintain improved performance, he or she is terminated.

Most of the clients we work with cannot afford to pay someone for six months to a year of low performance while this process unfolds, so they terminate the employee at the first recurrence of low performance following a PIP.

An organization can safely use either of these approaches or an iteration that balances the two. Whichever approach is chosen, it must be applied consistently to reduce risk and feelings of internal inequity.

5. I haven't terminated this individual yet because I dread having the conversation with him, and I'm concerned about the impact this could have on him. I know it's time to terminate, so how do I show him compassion and clarity?

Terminating an individual is an experience that should be treated seriously, but it doesn't have to be entirely negative. In our leadership experience, we learned that by being open about the reasons for termination and supportive of the individual's success going forward, it was actually possible to conclude a termination conversation with the individual feeling optimistic about the future. Not every conversation will end this way, but one particular mindset will help you increase the odds that it will.

The key to a successful termination conversation is truly believing that the individual's perfect job is definitely out there, but it's not on your team. This approach empowers you to respect the skills this person has to offer while staying objective about actual performance levels.

Every recommendation made in this section is a tool in a toolbox. Expecting to know how to use every tool right away is unreasonable. Set yourself up for success by leveraging the tools in the order they were introduced. The tools are designed to build on each other so that they are easier to employ and more effective when used successively.

Performance management is a holistic system, supporting skill development and line of sight. It should continuously raise the performance of all team members and also create exit opportunities for those who are not the right fit for the team.

Sometimes taking one single step toward a new system is the best way to build strength and confidence in your own skills. Schedule monthly check-ins with your team members immediately. Engage in a conversation about their performance and development goals. Then refer back to this section and choose a tool to implement the strategy that will best help your team achieve its goals.

Checklist for Implementing Individual Development Plans and Performance Improvement Plans

- Do some research within your network and on the Internet to find examples of successful IDPs and PIPs.

- Develop an IDP template for your team.

- Review your own goals to make sure you have the bandwidth to fully support your team's goals and development needs.

- Schedule quarterly check-ins for the IDP.

- Make sure your employment attorney has reviewed the PIP you plan to use.

- Outline a consistent approach to implementing PIPs to ensure that different managers don't use the PIPs in different ways or on different schedules.

- Bring cupcakes to celebrate completed development assignments and goal achievement!

Part V

Team Performance

Chapter 12

A-Players and Bad Apples

"There's at least one bad apple on every team, right?" We've heard this phrase more times than we can count. With one sentence, managers flippantly excuse shockingly low performance or frustrating behavior. What we find so incredible about this simple phrase is not only that it excuses the behavior, but also that the manager who says it obviously believes it. And because the manager believes it, he is willing to endure it—for years.

When we started writing this chapter, we considered beginning it with inspiring words about sparking greatness in team members. There are countless studies on employee motivation, and we're going to get to some of those, but the most important studies are actually those that are the least talked about—the studies that show again and again that the one bad apple is not only disrupting and demotivating your team, but also bringing down the performance level of everyone else on the team.

In 2006, William Felps of the University of Washington College of Business published "How, When, and Why Bad Apples Spoil the Barrel: Negative Group Members and Dysfunctional Groups." Felps's paper pulled together dozens of previous studies on teams and deleterious behavior. We'll get into the details—and believe us they are juicy details!—but the key takeaway from Felps's paper is this: "This personality-based research has found that how low the lowest teammate is on the variables of conscientiousness, agreeableness, and emotional stability is usually a strong predictor of group-level variables."[55]

This is a powerful statement cloaked in academic jargon. Felps is telling us that your team's performance can be predicted based on the lowest performer's level of conscientiousness, agreeableness, and emotional stability. If all managers understood that the lowest performer on their team set the performance bar, would they so flippantly dismiss the behaviors preventing the team from reaching its potential?

We'll admit, we found Felps's findings hard to believe at first. After all, a team of rainmaking rock stars isn't going to be brought down easily by one disagreeable, unconscientious person, right? Wrong. Let's take a closer look at why.

The Three Types of Bad Apple

Felps was not only kind enough to explain how one bad apple brings down an entire team's performance, he was also gracious enough to identify three specific types of bad apple so you can more easily identify which of the three is currently vexing your Wednesday afternoons. The three types Felps identified are the withholder of effort, the affectively negative individual, and the interpersonal deviant (our personal favorite based on name alone).

The Withholder of Effort

The biggest project proposal of the year is due in twenty-four hours, and all the team members, save one, are in a state of frenzied productivity, giving their all to ensure that the proposal leaves the prospective client in awe of a potential partnership. Where is the missing team member? Is she at home with a frightfully high fever? At her daughter's first dance recital? At her dying mother's bedside, surely.

A withholder of effort, by definition, regularly puts in far less effort than the rest of the team and somehow gets away with it. "Missing in action" is this individual's modus operandi.

"Withholders of effort produce feelings of inequity with no easy resolution in a team environment," notes Felps.[56] In other words, "if Mike is producing mediocre projects with plenty of defects, why am I burning the candle at both ends to produce excellence?" High performers will almost always come to resent that withholders of effort get the same role and rewards for less effort and often less and poorer quality output. High performers will almost always react by reducing their effort, caring less about the quality of their work, or looking for a team that offers recognition, rewards, and opportunity on par with their work product.

Withholding Spreads through a Team

We challenge you to consider for a moment what other factors beyond distraction or a penchant for loafing might contribute to a withholding of effort. Consider a time when you've worked with people who just didn't put in the time or never met their goals. What might explain their behavior other than mere laziness or complete lack of engagement?

The answer is a lack of skills or even general incompetence. If incorrect assumptions have been made about a team member's skill level, and expectations for that team member are based on those assumptions, then the individual's actual performance will fall well below the expected performance.

The individual will move at a slower pace than the rest of the team to reach targeted results, often requiring other team members to pick up the slack. If team members are asked to support the development of the team member, the time and effort they expend providing that support holds the team back from the achievement they would be capable of with an appropriately skilled individual. Understandably, this often leads to feelings of frustration and inequity in the high performers.

The Affectively Negative Individual

Did you know that your brain actually focuses on negative experiences more than on positive ones? Felps quotes Rein, McCraty, and Atkinson on how the brain responds to positive and negative experiences: "Whereas a positive emotion (i.e., compassion) wears off relatively quickly, researchers find that when they give someone a negative feeling (i.e., anger) to concentrate on, the physiological effects last over five hours" (Rein, McCraty & Atkinson, 1995)."[57] Our brains are hyper-focused on the negative as a matter of survival; our responses to negative experiences are disproportionately strong compared with our responses to positive ones.

Why Bad Experiences Count More than Good Ones

In a society so focused on happiness, it may seem counterintuitive that our brains are hardwired to focus on the negative. But evolutionarily, this focus on negative experiences helped humans avoid harmful situations. When the brain was still evolving into the computational powerhouse it is today, those who survived did so because negative experiences left such a strong impression that the individual never forgot them and, going forward, managed to avoid the situations that caused them. Our ancestors needed to dwell on a rival tribe's aggressive behavior to remember to avoid going near the tribe's territory, since staying alive was way more important than, say, employee engagement and job satisfaction. But in today's open-office environments, our neural hardware is, unfortunately, a bit out of date. Staying alive has become relatively easy in much of the world, so we focus on professional satisfaction. And in today's professional world, dwelling on the fact that a teammate treated you disrespectfully in a meeting four years ago doesn't aid survival, but instead leads to unpleasant and unproductive negativity.

To distill this down, affectively negative individuals hyper-focus on past grievances and dwell on how those experiences make them feel. They bring their persistent negative viewpoint, feedback, and emotions to the team, which eats away at productivity and morale.

The Interpersonal Deviant

Easily the most exciting label of the three, when our clients hear "interpersonal deviant" they always seems to conjure up images of a smarmy individual plotting complex and devious acts of sabotage. While the interpersonal deviant does not typically walk around stroking his chin and laughing villainously, this type of bad apple does consistently violate the norms and values the team has explicitly or implicitly set.

One banking client team hired us to bring their management practices, specifically in the area of accountability, to a new level, as they were poised for strong growth in the coming years. They knew that without clear accountability and employee development, chaos would ensue.

At the outset of the engagement, the banking client's guiding coalition outlined the following set of rules for their performance improvement work:

- prioritizing team performance meetings above all other work except client emergencies
- showing up to meetings on time
- completing fieldwork assignments
- having complete openness regarding opportunities for the organization to improve

The CEO personally invited one employee to join the team since she often had a different perspective from other team members. This type of counterbalance to a team can often be invaluable. It helps bring a holistic approach to work, and, by bringing up different experiences or concerns, ensures that the team doesn't start acting like lemmings, cheering and supporting each other right over the edge of a cliff.

This team member, one of the midlevel managers, didn't just think differently from the other members of the team, she knowingly and persistently violated the explicitly stated rules of the group. She was present at approximately 20 percent of the meetings, showed up late when she did attend, and never completed fieldwork assignments. As if these behaviors weren't frustrating enough, her response to the last rule was particularly interesting.

Many in this group had to find great courage to express their concerns about the future of the organization—after all, the group included the CEO and each of the top executives, in addition to midlevel managers. As you can imagine, it takes a confident midlevel manager to share performance observations and concerns with executives in a way that is open, authentic, and objective. The executives in this group supported these observations by regarding them as valuable and appreciated, setting the stage for true change in the future.

The interpersonal deviant in this group, however, would allow everyone else to speak their concerns and experiences first, then calmly state that she wasn't sure what everyone else was so upset about. "After all," she said to us, "we all have great jobs working for the best possible CEO. This is one of the best companies possible to work for and sure we have things we could work on, but I don't experience anything like what they are talking about and, personally, I just feel that our leadership could not do a better job."

Note her use of the word *they*. She often spoke of us as consultants and of the group as *they*—as if we and her fellow team members were a third party, which was alienating for everyone involved. Her perspective was entirely valid; she may truly have felt there was nothing the organization could do better. What violated this team's norms was the way in which she stated her opinion—she came across as passing judgment and chastising the other group members for daring to question the effectiveness of the organization. This delivery shut down some team members and put others on the defensive, derailing the culture of the team and slowing down the progress.

This individual's blatant, continuous violation of team expectations began to hijack productive meetings. Whether she was present or not, she prevented the team from feeling truly cohesive.

Preventing Performance

Psychologist Bruce Tuckman proposed (way back in 1965) that all teams go through four predictable phases together: forming, storming, norming, and, finally, performing. This team had spent years forming, storming, and norming. They weren't quite performing yet, which was one of the main objectives of our partnership with them. But the interpersonal deviant's continuous violation of the group's implicit and explicit norms was so jarring and triggered such negative emotional reactions that she ultimately prevented the group from finding its highest level of performance.

Comfort with accountability is already startlingly low among teams, but when we do find ease with the concept of accountability, it is almost always because technical skill is lacking or client results have been compromised. The three types of bad apple team members most likely bring behaviors to work that stem from habits formed in childhood. They live in the murky area of personality and interpersonal work misconduct that causes accountability squeamishness.

Because the results of these behaviors are sensitive to discuss and challenging to quantify, they escape feedback for years. And for all the years they escape feedback, they disrupt team cohesion and prevent top performance. The cost to the organization of allowing these behaviors to continue materializes in many ways: wasted time and energy on projects, team turnover, and, worst of all, lower productivity than is possible as high performers lose their motivation to do their best. Some clients we've worked with aren't at risk of failing, but they never quite achieve the level of success they envision. They also, almost unfailingly, refuse to address the major behavioral problems on their teams, never connecting a lack of accountability to lower than expected performance.

One of our favorite books on the art of powerful and persuasive communication, *Fierce Conversations*, demands that readers ask themselves a simple question of staggering implication: "What are you pretending not to know?" In order to be a best-in-class manager with a peak-performing team, you must stop pretending not to notice corrosive behavior.[58] No behavior that has a negative impact on other team members should escape accountability and coaching. The concept of "impact on the team" is exactly how you would frame any conversation about behavior with a team member who is showing signs of being a bad apple.

Bad apple behaviors occur outside of KPIs and goals. However, your willingness to keep your team clear of disruption places the responsibility for the consequences of the behaviors squarely at your feet. What you permit, you promote.

The previous section on individual performance precedes this section for a reason. We wanted you to clearly understand the accountability tools available to you when behaviors like this occur. By leveraging check-ins, performance journaling, and even a PIP if needed, you can actively coach your team members away from deleterious habits or, if necessary, remove them from the team.

Continuous Coaching

A change in behavior will not happen with one conversation, or two, or even three. Be prepared to offer continuous coaching to a team member who exhibits harmful behaviors, but also recognize when the negative consequences to the team outweigh a continuous investment of time.

If one or more of these three bad apple behaviors sounds all too familiar to you, it's time to take action. By identifying a pattern of behavior, its impact on the team, and how you need that behavior to change, you have the elements of a powerful and supportive coaching conversation. It's important to keep in mind that somewhere along the way, this behavior helped this person survive or succeed; unfortunately, it's not serving them or the team any longer.

Checklist for Preventing Bad Apple Behavior

- Know the three types of behaviors well.

- Keep an eye out for corrosive habits that you might have previously excused away.

- If you recognize that a team member is dysfunctional, begin observing the triggers of the dysfunctional behavior and see if you can identify a theme.

- Hold a conversation with the individual about the behavior and be prepared to coach this person to change the behavior.

- Be prepared to implement a PIP if the person does not consistently show improvement.

Chapter 13

A Growing Team is a Learning Team

"I feel like I'm drowning and can't ever get above the work to get some air." Jennifer has been managing her team of two for four months. After proving herself an excellent developer at her startup company, she was promoted to a manager position and charged with bringing four medium-size client projects to completion. When we began working with Jennifer, the projects were nowhere near being successfully completed. Jennifer has brilliant technical talent, bringing energy and passion to her work and her team. For some reason, however, no one on the team could make a major deadline.

Jennifer's team was not only suffering from burnout and frustration, but they were also creating a significant bottleneck for the rest of the organization. Jennifer's confidence was foundering and her team's confidence in her was going with it. "I was doing really well six months ago. My work was so great, I felt like I could accomplish anything thrown at me. Now, I feel like with every project, our team just gets farther behind and loses more confidence."

Like so many technically brilliant team members, Jennifer had been promoted to manager without any managerial-skill training or development. This meant she was tasked with a stretch goal (managing two other individuals and their work) without having the opportunity to develop the tools she needed to accomplish this goal (the skills to manage and motivate others).

As we peeled back the layers of frustration and complexity, it became clear that the entire team lacked time management skills. All three members failed to set clear deadlines or communicate the specific support they needed to complete their work in a timely manner.

As an individual contributor, poor time management didn't stand out as a problem in Jennifer's earlier performance management because she would occasionally pull all-nighters to meet deadlines, or more often than not, her managers gave her a few days of grace because her work was so strong. By not holding Jennifer accountable or teaching her how to effectively manage her work deadlines, Jennifer's managers set her up for failure in her new role.

Jennifer described the sinking feeling that comes from wanting to change her team's habits but having no idea how to do it: "My manager tells me that I need to manage my team's time better so that we make our deadlines. Trust me, if I knew how to do that, I would. She keeps telling me to get the team to change our habits, but I don't know what to do differently."

Jennifer's team has a skill gap that is preventing them from meeting deadlines and therefore diminishing the ability of the entire organization to reach peak performance. If we sound alarmist it's because situations like this are worthy of alarm.

Let's take a look at two highly effective team-learning tools before we bring Jennifer's story to a conclusion.

The After-Action Review

If an athlete wants to set a new personal record—say, a faster mile or a heaver deadlift—the athlete won't achieve the goal using the same approach she has been employing up to this point. Always remember: *What got you here won't get you there.* Write this aphorism on a sticky note and put it where you will see it every day. (While you're at it, order Goldsmith's book.) The saying is true for both individuals and teams. Simply setting a higher goal does not mean that the team has the skills to achieve it sustainably.

If, however, you identify the behaviors that need to change and grow in order to reach this new goal, you can put your team on a path toward building higher capacity through higher capability. Your team members will be prepared to take on larger and more complex responsibilities as they adopt a habit of learning from every major project and significant goal what did and did not work.

Changing the Culture of the United States Army

After the Vietnam War, the United States Army knew it had a very serious problem. Its training infrastructure was designed around an enemy that fought along clear battle lines, made themselves visible during combat, and maneuvered somewhat predictably. It makes sense that after fighting both World Wars this way, military hierarchy and training would focus on this style of warfare. But when this strategy was applied to the Vietnam War, it turned out to be a complete disaster. Our troops did not enter the jungles of Vietnam with what's now called "distributed intelligence." Rather, they attempted to fight guerilla warriors with a strategy of command and control.

The National Army Training Center (NATC) is the hub of the Army's learning and development. Every type of training, whether in a classroom or a tank, takes place there to give troops and their tactics the chance to engage in mock battle before they ever meet a foe. It was at the NATC that the post-Vietnam Army set about seeking ways to increase the capability and capacity of its individual troops and thereby its platoons. The outcome of this search was the creation of the after-action review, a team learning tool that research has shown increases team performance, efficacy, openness of communication, and cohesion.

The Army describes the after-action review as "a professional discussion of an event, focused on performance standards, that enables soldiers to discover for themselves what happened, why it happened, and how to sustain strengths and improve on weaknesses."[59]

Sustain strengths and improve on weaknesses. These are the very outcomes needed to bring Jennifer's team to the level of performance her manager knew was possible. The after-action review is credited with utterly transforming the culture and efficacy of the United States Army. So, yeah, it will most likely work for your team.

After-Action Review Detailed How-To

The after-action review consists of two statements and three key questions:

1. Describe the intended outcome (of the plan, the goal, the event, the meeting, etc.).

2. Describe the actual outcome.

3. What contributed to meeting the intended outcome? (What went well?)

4. What detracted from meeting the intended outcome? (What didn't go as well as it could or should have?)

5. What did we learn that we will apply in the future in order to achieve our intended outcome?

The beauty of the after-action review is its habit-forming simplicity. It can take place in the car after a sales meeting, during a regularly scheduled team check-in, or it can be its own team event. The point is that whether an after-action review lasts five minutes or five hours, research has shown that it has a significant impact on a team's ability to continually learn and improve performance.

The Center of Military History's fascinating book, *A History of Innovation: U.S. Army Adaptation in War and Peace*, describes the after-action review as one of the most disruptive, vital innovations ever to emerge from the NATC.

The after action review was probably the single major influence on the revolution in training that took place in the Army in the twenty years following the Vietnam War. The National Training Center established it as a formal and valuable method and helped propagate the review process as an evaluation tool throughout the Army by the mid-1990s. The center's observer/controllers conducted reviews at platoon, company, and battalion levels as well as for supporting elements.

More than one battalion commander found the reviews to be "brutally honest." Reporters characterized the process as "a military group therapy session" and "a warfare class for the MTV generation." Another correspondent came closest to capturing the contribution the after action reviews made to improved training:

"Sir," the young lieutenant begins, "I don't really think the commander made clear exactly what his intent was." After a moment's uncomfortable silence, Gen Barry McCaffrey, then commander of the 24th Infantry Division, speaks up. "That's a good point," he acknowledges. "Getting our purpose across is key." Suffice it to say that ten years ago, a young Army officer was just as likely to commit hara-kiri as to openly criticize his commanding officer.[60]

Now, back to our athlete. A runner who wants to increase his mile time could simply bump up his practice time—consistently practicing and consistently failing to identify opportunities for improvement. If, however, that same athlete conducted an after-action review with his coach after each practice drill, research shows that the athlete would be far more likely to incorporate the miniscule and yet incredibly significant running habits that differentiate the great from the best.

The after-action review embeds a feedback loop into every goal, every project, and every occasion worth learning from. The beauty of the habit is that with leaders' consistent reinforcement, the tool itself starts showing up regularly on an informal basis. The increase in performance and cohesion resulting from the after-action reviews spurs the team to engage in more reviews, starting a *virtuous* cycle of continuous improvement and capacity building.

Avoiding Pitfalls

In our experience there are three key ways to negate the effectiveness of after-action review immediately. Bookmark this page and be sure to avoid each one of these during your first review!

1. The leader creates a highly defensive environment, preventing honest feedback. This can include post-review consequences and small retaliations for engaging in constructive dialogue. Without a safe and open environment, after-action reviews are a waste of time.

2. In response to the final question, "What did we learn that we will apply in the future in order to achieve our intended outcome?" the team may list three or thirty behaviors that need to change in the future. If the team commits to changing thirty behaviors at once, it's setting itself up for failure, which creates a loss of faith in the process. Be realistic when deciding how to act on responses to the third question, and be sure to hold teams members firmly accountable for the decided-upon changes in behavior.

3. On the flip side, if a team goes through the after-action review then fails to commit to any changes, the exercise is again a waste of time. This review offers very specific calibrations for incremental improvement that add up to major improvement over time. If the adoption of new behaviors is never taken seriously from the get-go, the team won't be taking long-term performance improvement any more seriously.

Occasionally during the after-action review, a negative outcome, large or small, will arise as a result of ordinary team behaviors. All too often, this negative outcome is a continuous frustration, popping up at regular intervals. In the worst cases, it's due to one person who lacks one or two key skills, which forces everyone around them to compensate by taking on more work to keep the wheels of the team moving smoothly. In order to preserve team respect for the after-action review process, it's crucial that the team leader listen closely to this feedback and address it accordingly.

Root Cause Analysis

Until a team actually confronts the true cause—the *root cause*—of a problem, the negative outcome will undoubtedly continue. The challenge is twofold: 1. Root causes can sometimes be tricky to identify. While some are as obvious as a leaky pipe causing constant slips and trips, others are hidden and require some Sherlock-style deductive reasoning. 2. Root causes, like accountability, can be scary. Sometimes the root cause of the problem really is that your colleague Mike is the perfect blend of irrational and jerk. If Mike's behavior is the true reason meetings are completely ineffective, it can be uncomfortable to identify that and *actually do something about it.*

So, the bad news is that you do have to dig deep and identify a root cause before you can solve a problem once and for all. The great news is that once you've found it, you can stop wasting precious hours on it and get on to more important things, like more after-action reviews.

As consultants, we take a perverse joy in witnessing the *symptomatic fixes* individuals employ to avoid dealing with root causes. One employee did her work huddled on a stepladder in the stockroom to avoid the Chatty Kathy in the office. A foreman never scheduled two brothers on the same job for fear a fistfight would break out. And one CEO took on hours of administrative work because a long-time employee beloved by the organization just couldn't complete it accurately, and the CEO couldn't bear to let her go.

You get the gist. Symptomatic fixes are workarounds that allow people to avoid addressing the fundamental problem, but in the end symptomatic fixes create other adverse side effects. Employees get frustrated about having to bear an extra burden. Toxic behavior that's allowed to fester can destroy the carefully built culture, or money is wasted on employees who don't actually fulfill their job expectations.

Symptomatic fixes often go hand in hand with a lack of accountability. When leaders fear that accountability will create conflict or rock the boat, they often respond with a symptomatic fix. We know leaders who, rather than focusing on the root cause of consistent missed deadlines, create fake earlier deadlines, which eventually erodes their staff's trust. We also know leaders who allow team members to abstain from working together if they have interpersonal difficulties. We know of a team that allows one particular member to work directly through management, even though the entire company is team based, because so many other team members have asked never to be paired with him again.

When a team is ready to reach a new level of performance, as demonstrated by their desire to self-reflect and change their own habits, the first step is to identify the root causes of performance-inhibiting behaviors. The after-action review supports a list of behaviors needing review. Root cause analysis is the tool that ensures you are addressing the *problem*, not the *symptom.*

Root cause analysis takes many forms ranging from simple to incredibly complex. In the safety industry, root cause analysis is a specialty all its own. The 2010 Deepwater Horizon oil spill illustrates why root cause analysis is such a valuable tool. With billions on the line and fingers pointing in all directions, root cause analysis essentially points a flashing neon arrow that says "accountable" at the responsible party.

The Five Whys

For the purposes of your team's improvement, we are going to teach you the most basic version of root cause analysis. Sometimes simple really is best, and the Five Whys method, which originates from the Toyota Production System (an oft-referred to model for continuous improvement), is elegantly simple. It's a quick exercise in which you work backward from the problem to the root cause by asking up to five *why* questions.

We often use a whiteboard to do the Five Whys exercise with a team. We start by writing a brief summary of the problem on the right side of the board. We ask a *why* question and list the responses on the left side of the board. We continue asking *why* questions up to five times until, based on the group's responses and analysis, we hit upon the root cause. On a whiteboard it looks something like this:

Why? #5 -> Why? #4 -> Why? #3 -> Why? #2 -> Why? #1 -> Problem

Solving a Performance Mystery with the Five Whys

We worked with a construction CFO and staff member who were struggling to address the staff member's sudden turn toward inaccuracy. In her five-year career, the staff member had never presented inaccurate reports to the CFO. But the CFO, who ran spot checks on all the reports, began noticing inconsistencies. Pretty soon, the CFO was finding that reports were inaccurate up to 20 percent of the time, a completely unacceptable number.

The CFO, not knowing to look for the root cause, applied a typical symptomatic fix: she began reviewing the accuracy of every single aspect of every single complex report. This took up to two hours *every week.* She would flag the inaccuracies and work with the staff member to dissect each mistake. They set targets of 90 percent accuracy, then 85 percent accuracy, but to no avail. Both parties were frustrated, and the staff member was understandably concerned about losing her position.

We sat down with both parties to conduct a root cause analysis. The results, which were surprising to everyone, included the following:

Problem: The staff member is experiencing a sudden decrease in accuracy.

Why? #1: "I've noticed that I've been making more mistakes as the field work has been ramping up and the project managers are interrupting me throughout the day."

Why? #2: "When they interrupt me, I pause in the middle of my concentration to help them, and I've noticed it's when I go back to the work after the interruption that I've often missed something."

Why? #3: "The expectation in the office is to be ready and available to support the project managers at all times. The implicit rule is that their questions take priority over my day-to-day work. The problem is that the increased level of questions is resulting in an increase in errors for me."

When we finished the third *why*, both parties had their own "aha" moment. We had hit upon the root cause. The cultural norm of the organization was that administrative staff were supposed to prioritize the needs of the projects over their own work. This makes sense since the projects were the revenue pipeline for the company. However, given that science has proven definitively that multitasking is ineffective, it's clear that giving administrative staff an uninterrupted block of time to complete their work would benefit everyone. If the project management staff were having this great an impact on this employee, what about the rest of the administrative staff?

Together with the CFO, we outlined a plan. The staff member would leverage the following tactics to minimize interruptions while maintaining a high level of support to project management staff:

- Procure a small whiteboard for her office door and write messages on it such as, "I'm working on financials from 2 to 4 today. Please feel free to email me your questions, and I'll return with an answer by tomorrow."

- Use her calendar to schedule chunks of time for focused work and make this schedule transparent on her calendar.

- Encourage project managers to email her with questions, assuring them they will receive a response within twenty-four hours. If a response is needed sooner, tell the managers to include "urgent" in the subject line.

Employing these tactics reduced the staff member's interruptions dramatically. Her accuracy went back to normal, and the project management staff was happy to help her be as efficient as possible.

Had this root cause gone uncovered, it's possible the staff member would have lost her job. She would have felt powerless against a continually increasing queue of questions and would have continued to lose confidence as her work suffered more and more. Finding the root cause stopped the vicious cycle and also helped the organization learn how it could communicate more effectively as it grew in size.

Both the after-action review and root cause analysis can be completed during an informal conversation between individuals or during a formal meeting with an entire team. The after-action review is best when used often; the team leader should conduct these reviews with an individual or a group *at least* once per quarter.

Root cause analysis is typically used more rarely. It may follow an after-action review if the team identifies a trend that needs to change. These two tools can be used together or completely independently of each other.

Removing Performance Obstacles

Let's circle back to Jennifer's team and their difficulty in completing projects on time. We conducted a root cause analysis with Jennifer's team and identified a lack of accountable communication and follow-up on Jennifer's part, leading to ambiguity and a lack of cohesion on the part of the team members.

When beginning a project, Jennifer did not always communicate the project's deadline. Even if she did, she did not schedule any check-ins to ensure her team was on track to meet the deadline, nor did she complete her own tasks on time. In general, Jennifer treated deadlines as suggestions when she should have treated them as rules.

The team, including Jennifer, were horrified at being considered a bottleneck in the organization, and they expressed relief and gratitude when the COO offered to help them implement and embed solid time management tools into their project management. The team's first experience with an after-action review was admittedly challenging. The second question, "What didn't go as well as it could or should have?" created a laundry list of time management don'ts.

Jennifer and the COO took an open, positive approach to the process. They reminded the team members, and each other, that not everything would change overnight, but week by week, they would be laying the foundation for stronger project management, and then their after-action reviews would focus more on higher level learning. We are thrilled to report that this is exactly what occurred. The team increased its time management ability and trust in learning together, sharing feedback with one another on a daily basis, and holding each other accountable to the new methods.

Creating an elegant virtuous cycle, the ongoing after-action reviews created the perfect forum for calling out any lapses in commitment to time management, further reinforcing the practices. The after-action review is a powerful tool for uncovering opportunities for improvement, but its ability to embed newly adopted practices is indispensable.

The next section tells the true story of a team turnaround that employed many of the skills and tools we have thus far outlined and was so spectacular that the company's own leadership was shocked by its results. Enjoy!

Case Study: Total Turnaround

Larry Peck had just seven weeks to turn his team's performance around or lose the company's biggest client, a national home improvement store. Peck had been with the endangered company for less than a year when he started to recognize major process and communication inefficiencies that were creating massive quality problems. The company specialized in the fabrication and installation of custom granite countertops and enjoyed a lucrative contract with the national retail chain. Three months into Peck's tenure with the company, that contract was threatened as installation quality increasingly declined month after month.

Rapid performance improvement was needed to save the company from potential ruin. Peck possessed the knowledge, willingness, and discipline to tackle the deep, systemic team issues. When the performance improvement effort began, the installation team's success rate on custom countertop installations was only 50 percent. For the other 50 percent, the team had to go back to make repairs, costing the company massive amounts of overtime as well as their reputation with clients.

While Peck recognized that the platform beneath the company was burning, the executive team did not feel the heat. They were very comfortable with the organization's status quo and were not in favor of any process change, despite the critical need for it.

To get broad buy-in from both executives and the workforce, Peck had to establish a clear sense of urgency. He recalls that "this event happened during one of the worst recessions in the construction industry. Revenue was drying up quickly, with no hopes of a quick recovery. The overhead was an anchor, instead of a life preserver. If something was not changed and changed quickly, the company would be out of the already scarce supply of cash and credit. The workforce had low morale. The product was OK at best. We were going to close in six months if we could not significantly improve our process."

Peck was promoted to head of operations six months after joining the company. With the company's largest client threatening to cancel its contract and a dire situation facing them, executives finally gave Peck the green light for a rapid performance improvement plan six months after his promotion. By the time Peck was given the go-ahead, nine months had passed since the contract was first threatened and Peck had begun sounding the organizational alarm. It took almost a year for the executive team to truly hear Peck and accept the sense of urgency, and now the team needed to act fast.

Although Peck had the know-how to lead the rapid improvement effort and now had the authority to do it, both the executives and the workforce eyed him and his plan with a heavy dose of skepticism. "Nobody knew how much improvement was possible. Who were we to think we could go from worst to best? Others had failed before. The people on the team had heard the talk about things getting better before, but had given up that it would ever happen, since it had not happened in the last twenty years. Failing to meet the goal would crush future improvement projects."

Knowing the company's solvency and any future improvement efforts were on the line, Peck took the authority given to him and began to rally the workforce toward creating a change vision.

At the beginning of the performance improvement effort, Peck was enrolled in a Six Sigma Black Belt course. The training he was receiving gave him a solid framework and foundation upon which to bring the workforce together, create a vision of higher performance, rework the necessary processes, and then finally "refreeze" the change into the company culture and everyday practices.

Peck formed a guiding coalition with a team of eight installation-crew supervisors. He then leveraged their expertise to create the change vision. He knew that any performance improvement goals defined would require the guiding coalition's buy-in. With the ultimate goal of maintaining company solvency by retaining the biggest client, the guiding coalition set the performance improvement goal of achieving perfect installation 80 percent of the time—a big first step given the current 50-percent level. The motto of the performance improvement effort became "Do it right the first time."

The team faced a number of serious obstacles, including an astonishingly short time frame, a lack of buy-in from a few key installation supervisors, ethnic and racial tension among some crew members, and language barriers between the fabrication crews and installation crews.

Any one of these obstacles could have derailed the performance improvement effort. Knowing what we now know about why the brain holds onto the status quo, overcoming the last three obstacles, which were deeply ingrained in the individual crewmembers, would require compelling reasons and strong leadership. Some members of the guiding coalition had been executing installations the same way for over twenty years. Without properly preparing for change and consistently supporting it with accountability, the company would not survive another six months.

Peck knew the stakes and was determined to bring discipline, accountability, and support to the process. This team leadership approach, combined with the knowledge and experience of the crews, resulted in astounding success. The installation performance improvements secured the client contract and ensured the company's continued survival.

Team Performance

Peck and the team leveraged the tools we have outlined in the Organizational Performance, Individual Performance, and Team Performance chapters to achieve their rapid success. In particular, regular opportunities for sharing feedback combined with constant after-action reviews resulted in an impressive upward spiral of team learning and increasing optimism.

Here are the four key elements of the team's success:

1. A clearly defined goal and the metrics to support it

The team defined success as completing 80 percent of installations perfectly the first time. "Perfectly" meant that no crewmembers would need to go back to the installation site to follow up or make repairs. The core metric watched by the team was the number of "go-backs" made by the crew each week. By decreasing this number, the team would get closer and closer to its overall goal of completing 80 percent of installations perfectly the first time.

According to Peck, "the mantra of the team became 'Do it right the first time.' This created a very clear line of sight for each employee—they understood exactly how small errors along the production chain could expand into huge problems down the line. Everyone started thinking seriously about how to do it right the first time—how they could do their small, individual piece right the very first time."

2. A discipline of regular check-ins

The guiding coalition met twice a week for two hours at a time to plan the performance improvement, share feedback, conduct after-action reviews, and discuss next steps. Peck also met with each member of the guiding coalition individually once a week. The full team of installers and fabricators met daily to share feedback, experiences, and ideas for process improvement.

More than once when discussing the performance improvement, Peck singled out discipline as key to the success of the effort. The discipline of the scheduled check-ins built momentum for change, which in turn facilitated company-wide adoption of the performance improvement goal and acceptance of the increased accountability needed to ensure the performance improvement effort was successful.

As Peck found, team enthusiasm for regular check-ins is often lacking at first. "The only reason the team showed up to the meetings was because it gave most of them a break from the daily grind. For the first couple of meetings, I had to personally collect bodies. It was only after the first perfect install of a large project that the magic happened. The high-fives and teamwork kicked in in a way that one would not have believed two months earlier."

While this substantial investment of time every week may not be required for all performance improvement efforts, Peck's decision to devote so much time to the performance improvement effort was critical to its success. A compressed time frame of seven weeks demands faster learning, planning, and procedural change, and that is impossible without face time and dialogue. Peck's intensive check-in schedule was perfect for this effort.

3. Persistent sharing of feedback

Peck knew that the crew had the knowledge and ability to reach their target, but they had to coach each other to reach it. "Informal feedback began to happen pretty quickly. Team members began helping each other. It was amazing to watch... by keeping feedback constantly going, it became easier for people to provide and receive it. If one only gets feedback occasionally, and that feedback is bad, it becomes very hard to have feedback conversations."

Each of the three regular check-in meetings required feedback from both management and the crew. The feedback might include success stories, lessons learned, or entirely new ideas on how to approach a current process.

One of the major drivers of morale for the performance improvement effort was the feedback from homeowners. The national retailer that contracted Peck's company for the countertop installations collected homeowner feedback about their installation experience and satisfaction. Over the course of the seven-week rapid performance improvement, the feedback from homeowners went from mediocre to glowing. The crews began posting the homeowner feedback forms on a wall so that every day they could be reminded of the progress they were making and the satisfaction they were leaving behind at the end of a successful installation. According to Peck, "having feedback conversations regularly creates an environment of mutual support where the point is not to blame or criticize, but to improve and assist."

4. After-Action Reviews

A defining characteristic of the team's transformation was the tenacity with which they pursued constant calibration. Peck describes a team willingness to pull together each and every time a "go-back" detracted from their 80 percent goal: "After several successes, a failure was heartbreaking, and a lot of energy was spent trying to figure out how to avoid the same failure in the future." As soon as a "go-back" was completed and the installation finished, every single team member associated with installation, from the sales representative to the fabricator to the installer, gathered together for an informal after-action review to identify the root cause of the problem. Outcomes from these reviews always included team learning and often included recommendations for process improvements.

Peck described this team learning process as critical for individual ownership of the improvement effort. He also notes that as teams worked together to uncover the issues leading to "go-backs," trust in each other was built through "not judging mistakes."

Rapid Improvement Success

If you have any doubts in your mind about whether these performance improvement tactics work, let this case study put them to rest.

Peck's rapid performance improvement effort yielded a complete turnaround for the team and for the company. If you recall, the two primary goals were to

1. Keep the company solvent by saving an endangered relationship with its largest client

2. Increase the rate of installations completed correctly the first time from 50 percent to 80 percent

The actual results far surpassed even Peck's performance hopes:

1. The team increased the rate of installations completed perfectly the first time to 92 percent.

2. Materials consumption was reduced by 50 percent, or 20 percent of revenue.

3. The national retail client not only renewed the contract, but also gave the company a national award of excellence for performance that was better than any other vendor in the country. (However, the company never again achieved exclusive supplier status, a cost of leaving the relationship endangered for too long.)

4. Employee morale and motivation increased markedly.

5. The entire company wanted to find more targets for performance improvement, and Peck led another four improvement projects during his time with the company.

Would you have believed such dramatic change could take place in just seven weeks? Before meeting Peck, we wouldn't have. When we interviewed him for this book, we realized that Peck had taken his team through every performance improvement step we recommend, with the team going through every phase of resistance, buy-in, and success that we predict will normally occur over the course of months. With so much at stake, Peck was able to invest a substantial amount of time and resources in order to achieve a much faster transformation.

What still resonates for us about Peck's story is how it illustrates what is possible from a team that has a passionate leader, change preparation, discipline, and accountability.

The story becomes all the more inspiring when you pause to take into account the sheer number of obstacles working against this change effort. Comfort with the status quo, racial divisiveness, a historic lack of discipline, and an astonishingly short time frame could have proved insurmountable without Peck's leadership and execution approach. Take some time to think about the obstacles to your performance improvement and ask yourself if they are truly as insurmountable as they seem.

A New Culture of Accountability

This dramatic performance improvement would not have been possible without an increase in company accountability. All too often when we bring up the topic of accountability to leaders and managers, we receive a circle of uncomfortable looks from the conference room table. While it's widely accepted that accountability is critical for high performance, the word *accountability* has not escaped a negative connotation. For many, accountability brings up mental images of dressing-downs and inescapable conflict. Unfortunately, this misperception of accountability is exactly what keeps it from being effectively leveraged to create a positive and high-performance team culture.

Peck recognized the presence of this negative perception of accountability and worked to dispel it: "I had to create an atmosphere that was both accountable AND nonjudgmental, which means making sure that everyone is collectively accountable to the greater group goal, rather than to protecting themselves from criticism."

During the performance improvement process, one particular job was started by one installation crew and finished by another. During the install, the countertop got dropped onto a one-piece, seamless floor, damaging it irreparably. Each team blamed the other, and suddenly Peck had the perfect opportunity to demonstrate that accountability does not have to be negative, but can instead result in a positive outcome and learning for everyone. "We were finally able to get the person who actually dropped the countertop to tell us what happened. As result, we implemented a new protocol for covering the floors with thick cardboard so the lifters could rest the top during a long carry. The person who originally owned up to the mistake was then congratulated for bringing this pervasive problem to the attention of the group so the issue could be solved for everyone."

Note the absence of humiliation, termination, or discipline. Yes, sometimes discipline is necessary. But much more often, Peck's style of accountability increased performance by creating learning opportunities and then doggedly pursuing desired results.

If you find yourself uncomfortable with the thought of increasing accountability, ask yourself whether you fear creating conflict or introducing negativity to the team. Neither conflict nor negativity is necessary to get the results you and your team are seeking. When you ensure that your team is leveraging the three key factors of accountability, you create an environment for learning, results, and continuous improvement.

Part VI

Leadership Performance

Chapter 14

Up Your Leadership Game

As a team leader, you have more at stake than ever before. Never in history has such a high level of transparency and knowledge sharing been possible. This means that your customers and clients have only to do a quick Google search to find a competitor after a single poor experience, and LinkedIn presents your top talent with an array of enticing new opportunities every day.

It's not unusual for today's employees to keep their resume current in case a friend recommends an interesting new opportunity. Imagine your VP of sales in line for her daily Starbucks, perusing her LinkedIn app for exciting sales positions at companies within a fifty-mile radius from home.

Ten years ago, would you have predicted that every single one of your team members would have a personal brand? Through social media and an intense focus on networking, today's high performers are always prepared to seek a different position if it offers greater development, a more intriguing challenge, or the opportunity to work for a stronger coach.

If you want to bemoan a shifting demographic and decreasing workforce loyalty, go ahead—we'll give you a minute. But that's all. You don't have time to lament a changing employment landscape because you need to start working on your plan to take advantage of it.

It's not just the talent landscape that's rapidly changing; an avalanche of new research into effective leadership has for the first time allowed us to understand exactly which leadership behaviors elicit success from teams. For those willing to put in the work, becoming a world-class leader is not a question of how, but when.

New Leadership for a New Era

Interestingly, the heaviest lifting needed to reach a new level of leadership doesn't start with commanding others; it starts, instead, with how we command ourselves. In a world that runs on email and 140-character statements, what today's high-performing employees are really looking for is connection with their team leader. This connection, forged in mutual respect and two-way feedback, is the foundation for employee engagement. Gallup, the world's foremost researcher on engagement, defines *employee engagement* as the condition in which employees are psychologically committed to their jobs and likely to be making a positive contribution to their organization.[61]

The take-no-prisoners approach to leadership, with its commanding tone, black-and-white viewpoints, and singular vision, was at one time revered as the embodiment of strong leadership. This style is often referred to as "command and control," and we're sorry to tell you that it just won't get you very far with today's high performers. Today's top talent aren't looking for Patton; they're looking for Marc Benioff, the Salesforce founder who takes the time to mentor up-and-coming talent, generously donates to a number of social causes, and recently stated in a *USA Today* interview that the United States needs to adopt a more "compassionate capitalism."[62]

In an era of increasingly virtual communication, digital solutions, and cutthroat competition, today's leaders and companies can set themselves apart as talent developers. How well your current talent speaks of you to their colleagues and friends often determines who comprises your applicant pool. How well you develop and manage your network of direct reports influences your future talent pipeline. This means that your leadership needs to be more than strategic and more than visionary; in order to stand out today, you need leadership that's *emotionally intelligent.*

You may be wondering what territory we've just wandered into. After all, we've just spent five sections of this book discussing strategy, performance measurement, and accountability. What does emotional intelligence have to do with getting your team back to growth? Absolutely everything.

Let's hit rewind and go all the way back to 1995. Boyz II Men and Bryan Adams are topping the music charts and Daniel Goleman has just published *Emotional Intelligence*, which will prove to be the beginning of a sea change in management. Goleman marketed his book by comparing emotional intelligence to IQ, and by making the claim that emotional intelligence can actually take an individual farther than a high IQ. For twenty years now, researchers have been testing this hypothesis, and time and again, they have found that Goleman was correct. In terms of salary and advancement, emotionally intelligent leaders come out on top.

So, what *is* emotional intelligence exactly? Unlike IQ, which can be tested and measured, what constitutes emotional intelligence is still being researched. Strong areas of consensus, however, have emerged. According to Goleman, psychologists such as "E.L. Thorndike were researching what they called 'social intelligence' as far back as the 1920s. Thorndike wrote an article for *Harper's Magazine* that defined this type of intelligence as 'the ability to understand others and "act wisely in human relations."'"[63]

Yale psychologist Peter Salovey organized the concept of emotional intelligence into five key areas of practice:

1. Knowing one's emotions
2. Managing emotions
3. Motivating oneself

4. Recognizing emotions in others

5. Handling relationships[64]

In 2009, Travis Bradberry and Jean Greaves published *Emotional Intelligence 2.0*, which expanded on Goleman's ideas. Here is just a sampling of their data:

- Of employees studied, 90 percent of high performers are high in EQ. Conversely, only 20 percent of low performers are high in EQ.

- People with high EQ make on average $29,000 more per year than people with low EQ.[65]

We have always approached executive coaching with the goal of increasing emotional intelligence. Interestingly, to many of our clients, the concepts listed above seem simple—kid's stuff. "Man, had I learned this when I was a kid, my life would have been really different" is a common response to these basic, yet deep concepts.

The great news is that all that money you paid your therapist was actually an investment not only in your mental and emotional well-being, but in your career as well. In talking through your emotions and coming to understand why your parents' neuroses trigger you to this day (nope, you aren't alone), you were actually doing the necessary work to master the first two key areas of emotional intelligence practice.

Achieving Business Success through Emotional Mastery

Emotional intelligence is a lifelong practice; there are always opportunities for growth because our world and the relationships in it are unpredictable. It's also important to note that the five areas of practice are not mutually exclusive; they are more like cumulative levels of continually increasing complexity. After all, imagine trying to effectively handle relationships, especially sticky ones at work, without first knowing your own emotions, and more specifically, your own triggers.

If you've never had the opportunity to witness leaders who have zero insight into their own feelings but act as though they are in complete control, trust us, it's not a pretty sight. The phrase "bull in a china shop" comes to mind. We've seen personal, pointed sarcastic remarks fly like arrows from a leader's mouth, only to have the leader later brush it off with, "Oh, I don't mean any harm, they know me." We've seen leaders fly off the handle then yell "I'm not angry or upset!" Uh-huh, yeah, okay.

In either case, employees treat these predictable and exasperating behaviors as they would treat any other bad apple. They either put a protective barrier of physical and psychological space between themselves and the leader, preventing the deep, authentic, strategic dialogue needed for success, or they self-select out. Guess who are the first ones to turn over? We'll give you a hint: It's not the other bad apples.

As the brilliant Yale psychologist Peter Salovey recommends, when we work to develop a leader's emotional intelligence, we start with the first area of practice, "knowing one's emotions." This is where you should start, too. No matter how many years you've been in psychoanalysis or how many personality tests you've taken in *Cosmopolitan* magazine, you still have work to do here.

In *The Happiness Hypothesis*, University of Virginia psychologist Jonathan Haidt introduces a simple, elegant metaphor to describe a complex system of neural connections: "the elephant and the rider." Essentially, the rider is the rational, analytical part of your brain, commonly referred to as your prefrontal cortex. The elephant is the emotional center of your brain, or your amygdala, which is stronger and more powerful but far less, um, logical, than the rider. The rider usually directs the elephant, but when the elephant is on a tirade, the rider loses control and holds on for dear life.[66]

Gaining Control Over a Wild Elephant

Here's what is so interesting about the power of the amygdala: From your infancy through adolescence, your amygdala—your elephant—learned what to fear and what should trigger a fight, flight, or freeze response. During this formative time, your brain is still growing and observing the world for patterns from which to create templates. These templates, which are essentially biases, serve as shortcuts for you as an adult. The problem is, these cognitive biases aren't always very accurate.

The human brain evolved to watch out for predators, angry tribe members, and dangerous situations. Now, it's more common for our brains to take the fight, flight, or freeze responses that dysfunctional family members hardwired into our brains and apply them unwittingly to a similarly dysfunctional boss. The fact that your boss's habits leave you fuming but don't bother your other team members isn't coincidence; it's brain science. The very things that caused you stress when you were younger now trigger stress for you as an adult.

Bradberry and Greaves elaborate further on trigger events in *Emotional Intelligence 2.0*: "When something generates a prolonged emotional reaction in you, it's called a 'trigger event.' Your reaction to triggers is shaped by your personal history, which includes your experience with similar situations."[67]

Wait, did we just take a detour down Psychotherapy Boulevard? Why yes, yes we did.

Let's take a moment to understand why we are rehashing Thanksgiving family dynamics in a team performance book. Emotionally intelligent leaders are statistically more likely to perform better than leaders with low emotional intelligence. In our experience, we have observed that emotionally intelligent leaders are much more likely to hold team members accountable, coach team members to higher performance, and be open to innovative ways of working.

These correlations aren't coincidence; they are neuroscience. As Goleman explains, "when [the amygdala] sounds an alarm of, say, fear, it sends urgent messages to every major part of the brain... And these [messages] are just part of the carefully coordinated array of changes the amygdala orchestrates as it commandeers areas throughout the brain. The amygdala's extensive web of neural connections allows it, during an emotional emergency, to capture and drive much of the rest of the brain—including the rational mind."[68] Team members choose what they will and will not communicate to their leader—that a huge customer just went to the competition, that they made a mistake in a huge proposal, that there is a much more efficient way to manage product ordering—based on whether or not they think you are going to react rationally and reasonably.

Have you ever triggered your manager? Accidentally walked into his emotional trip wire without even realizing it was there? He most likely reacted in a disproportionately angry, defensive, or even hurtful way, leaving you feeling like an unfortunate bug that just met the business end of a swatter.

If your manager's elephant ruled the rider on a regular basis, you know *exactly* how little enthusiasm you had for open and candid conversations with him. Given that this manager had so little self-awareness regarding his impact on you, did you find him to be an excellent coach, giving you plenty of accolades to pair with specific, truthful, timely feedback? We didn't think so. It's difficult to truly manage your relationships with others if you aren't aware of your own triggers and, therefore, are unable to manage your own reactions.

We have veered into neuroscience and psychology because at the end of the day, no strategy, KPI, or after-action review can trump the power of the amygdala. To be the best coach and accountability partner you can be, and to be resilient in the face of the ugly truth that sometimes your performance needs improvement, your rider *must* be ready to guide your elephant, even when it rears up in the face of a trigger. We're going to show you how.

The Pivot Process

Daniel Goleman gives us the first of many clues on how to successfully pivot from a triggered state to one far more conducive to leadership success: "The prefrontal cortex can refine or put brakes on the amygdala's impulse to rampage, but cannot keep it from reacting in the first place. Thus, while we cannot decide *when* we have our emotional outbursts, we have more control over *how long* they last."[69]

Many a psychologist has created methods for decreasing the impact of an emotional hijacking. We have distilled these methods into our own three-step process called the Pivot Process. It allows you to pivot from an emotionally hijacked state to one of rational thinking, allowing you to present your *best* self in the most trying of circumstances.

Step 1: Know Thyself

Have you ever been infuriated by someone cutting in front of you at the grocery store, only to realize hours later how ludicrous it was to act like a total jerk at Whole Foods? Why did you react so strongly? It's very difficult to decrease the impact of an emotional hijacking until you are aware *you are right now, in this moment, being emotionally hijacked.*

If you find yourself apologizing to your employees or spouse on a fairly regular basis for things you said when you were mad, this section is worth its weight in gold. If you ever find yourself feeling bad about how you reacted in the moment, it's because your amygdala was in control, reacting to a trigger that recalled stress or pain from long ago.

In order for your rider, or prefrontal cortex, to regain control, you first have to recognize your emotions have taken over *as it's happening.* This is tough to do and takes practice. But think about it for a moment. What if, as your hackles rise and you feel yourself getting hot under the collar, about to toss out the most perfectly barbed put-down, you recognize, "Wow! This is what it feels like when my amygdala takes over!"? You have just engaged your prefrontal cortex, which has allowed you to label the moment rationally, meaning your rider is back in the game!

You can master this Jedi mindset by increasing your awareness of when you are triggered. Some clients of ours start out recognizing a triggered state *weeks later.* Some, thanks to therapy, are already able to recognize their triggers in the moment; they just still feel stuck in the seductive thrall of their emotions. If you commit to recognizing when you are triggered, you will notice that the time it takes to call up your prefrontal cortex continually decreases until it actually springs into alertness in the triggered state. Now you are ready for the next step.

Step 2: Personal Archaeology

This next exercise takes *know thyself* to an even deeper practice. In the first stage, you are learning to recognize your emotions in the moment to prevent them from hijacking your more rational self. However, to decrease the power of your own triggered states, you need to understand what patterns trigger you in the first place.

While some triggers, especially traumas, can have adult onsets, the vast majority of triggers stem from childhood experiences and environments. As we discussed earlier, your brain is most malleable in childhood, when you observe the world around you learn to categorize things in adulthood as beneficial or dangerous. Our brains are like your organization-obsessed friend who drank one too many cups of coffee: They absolutely thrive on categorization and labeling. If your brain had to label something for the first time every time, we would never accomplish anything. During childhood, your brain learns shortcuts: Are people mostly fair or unfair? Do others care about me, or do I have to watch out for myself first, above all others? Am I worthy of love or recognition?

As Goleman explains, "the more ordinary travails of childhood such as being chronically ignored or deprived of attention or tenderness by one's parents, abandonment or loss, or social rejection may never reach the fever pitch of trauma, but they surely leave their imprint on the emotional brain, creating distortions—and tears and rages—on intimate relationships later in life."[70]

In order to take the teeth out of your triggered moments, you need to understand what stimulus your brain is misinterpreting as something negative from your past. Once you understand your own triggers and the emotional hijackings that result from them, you can start to fully appreciate why everyone has a different set, like fingerprints. Everyone has a different upbringing, and the differences result in wildly different responses to the world once we're grown up. It's why your spouse sometimes completely misinterprets what you say, or why you respond disproportionately when he or she forgets to compliment you in a certain way. Goleman describes why it can be so difficult to reset your reactions: "The emotional brain's imprecision in such [triggered] moments is added to by the fact that many potent emotional memories date from the first few years of life, in the relationship between infant and its caretakers... These emotional lessons are so potent yet so difficult to understand from the vantage point of an adult life because... they are stored in the amygdala as rough, wordless blueprints."[71]

Creating a Self-Awareness Shortcut

Only by understanding the themes present in your childhood can you understand what triggers you as an adult. Themes can serve as a shortcut to identifying triggers, allowing you to more efficiently recognize how your personal emotional memories may be coloring today's experiences. There are two great ways to begin uncovering these themes and organizing them. You can start by keeping a journal or list of your triggers, distilling them into themes such as unfairness, not being valued, fear of being unloved, disconnection, etc. Or, you can find a great therapist to help you go through the same process. Frankly, it's entirely possible to do this on your own, but with the right partner it can go even faster and you get the benefit of an objective guide.

Think of it this way: Your amygdala created software for interpreting the world. You need to hack into the coding to understand which reactions it's applying to which situations and why.

The personal archaeology step is all about increasing the role of rational thought. Just as labeling a triggered state requires invoking logic during an emotional hijacking, so does recognizing that the VP of finance triggers you because his judgmental commentary takes your brain back to your mother's nitpicking requires that your prefrontal cortex be ready to analyze the situation and sort it all out objectively. The simple act of applying this step helps you take back control of your thinking, reactions, and emotional state. In fact, after a lot of practice, the people who trigger us the most can often become those who offer us the most valuable lessons.

Step 3: Question and Engage

The third and final step requires that you ask yourself this very specific question: "What is the very best choice I can make right now to foster collaboration and learning?" When your spouse unwittingly prompts a triggered state, eliciting anger, frustration, or deeply hurt feelings, are you at your most gracious and loving? Is it typically your first instinct to ask, "Can you help me to better understand what you would like from me? I genuinely want to know." A vast majority of our clients laughed heartily at this question and answered with an emphatic *no*. They went on to explain their typical spouse-triggered responses, which included but weren't limited to door slamming, freezing out, and sarcasm.

Our triggers take us to a deeply egocentric state that focuses on the feeling of being a victim of a great injustice—even when that injustice is something as objectively minor as being cut off on the freeway. In this victim-oriented mindset, caring about how our triggering aggressors (read: coworkers and significant others) are feeling in the moment or wondering what may have led them to act as they did never enters our sphere of consciousness. Our main thought process is something on the order of "How DARE they [point out my typos/question me in a meeting/use all the coffee creamer]?!"

As you master the process of withdrawing from a triggered state, you will be able to both recognize the fact that you are triggered and label the emotional memories that provoke the state *while you are within the triggering event itself.* In real time, in the middle of a conversation, you are taking back control from your amygdala. "Victorious" doesn't begin to describe how wonderful it can feel to shatter the perspective you are applying to a situation in the moment and recreate it in a way that you know is more constructive.

The first two steps remove the triggered, skewed, and inaccurate view of the situation and allow room for the third step: learning more about the situation and acting as a partner instead of an adversary. As you back away from an emotional hijacking, your amygdala is going to be tempted to take back control. How you engage your prefrontal cortex—and the person in front of you—will determine whether you can fully shed the triggered state.

In our experience, the single best action at this juncture is to ask a question. The simple beauty of this action is that it works especially well when you're engaged in a challenging conversation, but it also works when the trigger is faceless, such as a dangerous driver or the person who denied you access to your first choice of university.

Let's take a look at employing this final step in a real scenario. You have two direct reports who are not responsive to email or voicemail and who have been ignoring your advice and feedback since you became their manager. Let's say one of your triggering themes is not being valued, which translates to your being triggered when you feel disrespected or not listened to appropriately. In your triggered state, you may respond emotionally, either lashing out at the two direct reports or feeling at their mercy and trying to win their approval. Neither of these responses is appropriate for a strong, high-performance leader, but both are often employed in cases such as these.

We would definitely recommend to any leader at this juncture to seek further information by asking a question. Schedule a meeting with each individual and be prepared to learn. Ask questions like, "what is preventing you from responding within our normal timeframe?" or, "I've noticed you have not implemented the tactics we spoke about last month—can you tell me about that?"

You may learn that your triggered instinct is correct, and your direct reports don't value you, in which case it's of the utmost importance that you handle the situation rationally rather than emotionally. Or you may learn that there is a true impediment to their meeting your expectations. We have seen direct reports implement a new tactic, encounter a snag, and immediately revert to old habits without discussing the situation with their manager. You may need to retrain your direct reports to come to you when an agreed-upon approach isn't working. Your reports may also have encountered a temporary work deluge, preventing them from prioritizing your communication over client communication. Either way, by engaging your prefrontal cortex to ask rational questions and engage in collaborative dialogue, you aren't missing out on the opportunity to learn about the factors getting in the way of your team's peak performance.

Leveraging the Power of Inquiry

The very moment you commit to inquiry and collaboration, you remove the power of emotional hijacking. Your perspective opens from narrow and self-centered to one that takes into account the needs and experiences of other people. You have released yourself from the shackles of an emotional hijacking and are prepared to lead from a place of logic and team focus, rather than from a fight, flight, or freeze mentality. By practicing this process, you can increase your emotional intelligence in each of the five areas of practice. Before they leveraged the Pivot Process, many of our clients had a difficult time getting past the "knowing one's emotions" step. After using this process, they were not only completely aware of their own emotions, but were also much more aware of and empathetic to others' emotions.

We coached one COO, Alex, who knew that his command-and-control style of leadership was stunting the growth of those around him. He didn't feel comfortable with his own leadership style, but he struggled to change his habits because he was strongly controlled by triggers. Growing up in a family that judged his academic career and personal behaviors harshly, his parents always made him feel that he never quite measured up to what they expected.

Driven by a relentless desire to achieve, Alex was young for his position by any standard. His drive, combined with his lack of core confidence, created a volatile leader. In particular, when direct reports brought him questions or ideas, Alex would feel frustrated that he either didn't have an immediate answer or that he didn't come up with the idea himself first. Consider this: Your direct reports are acting as stewards of the organization, taking it upon themselves to improve current processes and increase efficiency, but instead of celebrating your fantastic hires and their genius, you feel threatened. This was Alex's everyday leadership experience. Because he spent his entire childhood and adolescence trying to be good enough, he spent his entire adulthood trying to be good enough.

Alex's triggered states resulted in unfortunate behaviors. With his elephant in full control, Alex lashed out and snapped at his team members, responding sarcastically to their well-considered questions. It's no surprise his talented team stopped bringing him ideas, but it is a surprise they stayed on. Alex was smart enough to know that his leadership style would not build a high-performing team. He was self-aware enough to know that his reactions stymied team progress, but he was stuck on the second step, managing his own emotions. Introducing Alex to the Pivot Process and guiding him through it over the course of a year allowed him to learn to reframe each situation in real time.

Rather than seeing questions and ideas from his team as indictments of his intelligence, they instead became an opportunity for growth. Alex had to learn that he would never reach the end of his search for mastery, and that constantly seeking the golden cup of "You Have Arrived" was to be constantly disappointed. Not only did Alex learn to see the curiosity of his team as a strength, he also became more curious himself. Unafraid of seeming unintelligent, Alex actively sought to build his own knowledge base.

Damaged relationships take time to heal, and the bonds between Alex and his team were no exception. By using the Pivot Process, however, Alex not only mastered his own emotions, but also opened up emotional bandwidth to better appreciate the emotions of others. He became more empathetic, which engendered a deeper trust from his team than ever before. Alex was much more comfortable with this approach to leadership, and the incredibly positive response from his team was the proof he needed that he was on the right track.

We encourage you to practice the three steps starting today. Be patient with yourself. Emotional intelligence, like peak performance, is a lifelong pursuit.

Chapter 15

The Hardest and Best Conversation You've Ever Had

Why does the concept of accountability often seem loaded with dread and more than a twinge of negativity? Many of us consciously or unconsciously see accountability as a first cousin to conflict. If you are holding people accountable, aren't you pointing out something they are doing wrong? And isn't that inevitably going to lead to hurt feelings on their part? Will they cry or lash out? Or worse, will they leave?

In this final chapter, we are going to teach you the ultimate accountability tool, which leverages emotional intelligence and evidence-based tactics to turn accountability into a positive experience that develops both you and the person you are engaging, while very likely strengthening the trust and connection between you.

This tool is called the Transformational Conversation. Inspired by two of our favorite books, *Fierce Conversations* and *Crucial Conversations*, we spent years as leaders practicing how to engage others in accountability conversations that would leave both manager and direct report motivated and clear on next steps. We recognized that accountability is not a one-way street: employees need to be able to ask their managers for what they need and hold them respectfully accountable when they don't get it.

Remember, your top talent is with you because they are looking for development and growth. If you are uncomfortable guiding them, or are clearly not offering them a path to better performance, they won't stay for long. Unfortunately, even top talent sometimes has a difficult time hearing constructive feedback. When one of your top performers has a habit that must change, you'll find the Transformational Conversation a game changer.

The Transformational Conversation comprises seven steps that support the fourth and fifth elements of emotional intelligence—recognizing the emotions of others and handling relationships. By combining the Pivot Process and the Transformational Conversation, you have almost all of the ingredients needed for robust growth in emotional intelligence.

Use the Transformational Conversation when you recognize that something needs to change. If the current course is headed for irreversible negative consequences, if the status quo is preventing you from reaching the next level of performance, or if you just can't take one more uncomfortable team meeting, this is the tool for you.

Scripting Leads to Mastery

When you first start using this tool, it's vitally important that you not leave out a single step of the conversation. We recommend preparing a brief outline of each step of the conversation so that you become more comfortable with it. Our own experience and feedback from leaders confirms that scripting leads to a much more centered and powerful conversation.

As you build your emotional intelligence and learn to recognize your own and others' emotions almost instantly, the need to follow every single step and script conversations lessens. You'll know you have mastered this tool when you find yourself using individual pieces of it in daily conversation. When you reach that point, you will feel comfortable applying your newly acquired communication prowess by organizing a challenging conversation in the way that seems most appropriate to the situation.

Let's now take a look at the seven steps of the Transformational Conversation. As we take you through them, we're going to use the example of Emily, who sets herself the goal of completing her design work on client projects within a two-week window, but who consistently takes one or two additional days to finish.

1. Make an Observation

Note that it's "observation" *not* "accusation." Identify objectively aspects of job performance, attendance, inability to meet deadlines, or other counterproductive behaviors that you or anyone else in your position would have noticed.

This type of observation is the perfect tool for calling out negative attitudes or behaviors that aren't specifically addressed in the employee handbook but that nonetheless can destroy your team or client relationships. Personal favorites include eye rolling, sarcasm, excuse peddling, inappropriate joking, and passive-aggressive tendencies.

Example of an objective observation: "Emily, I've been noticing for the past few months that you let me know your projects are complete about one or two days after the agreed-upon deadline."

2. Share a Feeling

Remember back in elementary school when your third-grade teacher brought some appropriately diluted psychology into the classroom and taught you how to speak in "I" statements? Now is the time to pull that skill out and put it to good use. By making an "I" statement that centers on an emotion, you are once again refraining from judging, while increasing the meaning in the conversation.

Once emotions are at stake, a conversation becomes very real. Sharing your emotions about a problem ensures that the conversation is as much about the relationship as it is about the problem. You are offering your vulnerability in exchange for theirs. Great leaders get things accomplished *through relationships*, and strengthening relationships is exactly what this conversation is designed to do.

The most typical expressions at this stage of the conversation are "I'm worried," "I'm concerned," or "I'm fearful."

Example of sharing a feeling: "Emily, I'm concerned because your work is otherwise truly excellent. I'm worried that this pattern of lateness will overshadow other areas of your performance."

Note that Emily's boss didn't yet dive into the other consequences of her actions. There is space within the conversation to explore the other consequences in just a bit.

3. Share Mutual Responsibilities and Perspectives

To be specific, use a personalized version of the following: "I know I have contributed to this by [insert something you have or have not been doing that has systematically supported the undesirable behavior]. Do you think I'm on the right track here? Have you noticed this as well?"

Grab a highlighter, a flashcard, a permanent marker—whatever you need to focus your attention on this step. It is the most important step of the entire Transformational Conversation.

If the person you are attempting to engage in a Transformational Conversation has a tendency to be defensive and manages to evade the conversation without any ownership or commitment, you have not made headway in changing his or her behavior. Unfortunately, you've just reinforced this person's confidence that he or she can outmaneuver you with defensiveness if needed. Typically, it's at about this stage in the conversation that the individual is deciding whether to put up a defensive front.

So far you've done a great job of preventing an emotional suit of armor from being deployed by keeping the conversation even-

keeled and based around observations and your experience—
not judgment. You are acting from mutual ownership and
collaboration, a winning combination that sets the right stage
for even the most hardened deflectors.

Ancient Psychology: The Reciprocity Principle

You are now about to employ a phenomenon called the
reciprocity principle. This principle, made popular by author
and professor Dr. Robert Cialdini, goes something like this: As
we were evolving into highly social beings, those who were
cooperative and offered a more even balance of give-and-take
were more likely to survive and pass on their genes. In today's
terms, it means we are highly likely to return a kind gesture, a
favor, or even the gift of ownership in a challenging conversation. By sharing your responsibility—your ownership—first in
the conversation, before asking for it from your direct report,
you are offering something while simultaneously psychologically preparing them to offer you the gift of ownership as well.

Is it a trick? If this is a trick on anyone, it's a trick on you, the
team leader. As individuals, we often witness behavior in others
that we wish would change. But we almost always fail to
recognize how we contribute to the continuation of the
behavior. This step in the conversation forces you, the leader, to
put on a systems-thinking cap and imagine the various variables
at play that contribute to an ongoing trend.

For example, we were coaching a CFO who often experienced
the frustration of having others disrespect her boundaries and
take advantage of her time and generosity. She found herself in
the same position over and over again. Yet in her mind, it was
always the result of the other party's nefarious ways, never the
result of her sending "I'll help with whatever you need" signals.

One day she called needing some coaching on her first
Transformational Conversation. "My employee has now taken
nineteen days of vacation over and above what she has accrued.
She owes the company thousands in vacation, and I am done
with it. Absolutely done. She's crossed the line too many times."

We walked her through the steps, and when we got to Step 3 she could not see how she contributed to this pattern. We suggested that the employee probably believed it was acceptable to continue taking vacation days because the CFO signaled that it was. The CFO paused and said, "Oh… my role in this is that I *allowed* the pattern for all this time. I could have said something eighteen vacation days ago, but I haven't said anything." Precisely.

The best leaders see behavior as an outcome of a complex set of variables. By understanding more of the variables, you are in a much more powerful position to change the behavior.

Once you have shared your responsibility, your direct reports may jump in with theirs as well. Great! You are well on your way to a productive conversation. But they may not be.

If that happens, you can try to prompt the sharing of mutual perspectives by continuing with a version of "Am I on the right track? Have you given any thought to this as well?"

Example of sharing mutual responsibilities and examples: "Emily, I know I have contributed by not scheduling check-ins with you during your projects. I will make sure to do that from now on. Have you noticed this pattern as well? Have you had a chance to give any thought to it?"

4. Offer Silence

You've laid out an objective observation, bared feelings about the observation, and taken ownership of your own role in the situation you are seeking to change.

Your direct report is either now sharing his or her perspective or is sitting in silence. You now have one single directive: Shut. Up.

The vast majority of the thousands of people with whom we've shared this model rate this step as the most difficult. Remember, every step is present and in its place due to years of practice and research. Your silence at this stage is an offering of collaboration. Your direct report has not spent the past two or three weeks (or years) thinking about and preparing this conversation as you have. Do them a solid and give them at least a few dignified moments to process and catch up. Susan Scott, author of *Fierce Conversations*, calls this "letting the silence do the heavy lifting."[72]

Create space in the conversation for your direct report to step forward and share his or her observations, feelings, and ownership. You'll be surprised at the quality of conversation that comes from strategically applied silence.

5. Explore Consequences

Motivational interviewing is a technique used by doctors and psychologists to help patients overcome addiction. By asking the *patients* to describe the consequences of their ongoing behavior, rather than having the doctor run through the litany of consequences, the patients craft a much more personal story of their own need to change. This simple exercise motivates change much better than engaging in a one-sided conversation.

Use this technique to your advantage by asking your direct reports to describe what's at stake if their behavior remains the same. If the lack of depth or clear understanding of consequences in their response surprises you, it's a good indication that they aren't fully aware of how their behavior is affecting those around them.

At this time, you can either agree and support their list of consequences, or let them know what else is at stake that they have not yet considered.

Example: "Emily, can you tell me about the consequences of turning in projects late, and what might be at stake if this continues?"

Emily may respond with something akin to, "I know that it doesn't reflect well on my work or ability to manage projects, and it puts everyone else in a bind trying to wrap things up for the client in order to meet their timeline."

Emily's manager would in turn respond with, "You are absolutely right on both fronts. Most recently, however, because graphics had one less day to work on their portion of the project for the client, they had to choose between delivering the product on time or adding in the finishing touches we are known for. Being even a day or two late could put our reputation at risk with some of our best clients. I need you to understand how crucial our deadlines are."

6. State the Ideal Outcomes

Just as you asked your direct reports to explore consequences, it's a good idea to give them the opportunity to state their ideal outcomes before you do.

Imagine your direct reports have a goal of bringing in $250,000 in new business each quarter, but they've been bringing in half that for two quarters now. If *you* state that your ideal outcome is the $250,000 in new business, what are the odds that your direct reports will agree, even if they don't think they can hit anywhere near that number?

If instead you ask your direct reports what their ideal outcome is, and they say it's $170,000, you now need to figure out if that number is due to their skill level or to a legitimate external factor you haven't yet taken into account. Either way, it's better to be in this position than having your direct report agree to an unrealistic number—again.

Also, what if the ideal outcome includes a novel solution to a problem? In one case, an otherwise high-performing employee was late to work almost every day due to traffic. The company's culture had always been not to ask questions, just give write-ups—or worse. The new COO had a different approach. He asked the employee why she was late every day. It turned out that her daughter's school start time was just late enough to clash with the employee's scheduled start time.

The COO had engaged in the Transformational Conversation and had asked the employee what the ideal outcome was. The employee asked if she could start thirty minutes later and complete her day thirty minutes later, taking on the responsibility of closing up the building. There was no reason not to grant this accommodation to the employee given her track record, and the individual who normally closed up the office was thrilled to be free of the responsibility.

Stay open to the ideal outcomes proposed by your direct reports. If you are working on their behavioral improvement, they may know exactly what it is they need to arrive where you want them to.

Example of seeking ideal outcomes: "Emily, what would be your ideal outcome with regard to deadlines in the future?"

"I think it's possible that I need one to two more days to complete the projects to the level of detail that we are promising our clients."

"I have watched you work, and I know you have a higher level of skill than any designers we've had in the past. They were able to produce great work within the two-week window. How about on this next project, I work upstream to gain an extra two days, but I also work alongside you to schedule the work and help you identify ways to complete your work with the same level of quality but more efficiently? Also, once we dial in the schedule, I'll make sure to schedule a brief check-in with you about three days prior to the scheduled completion date so that we can make sure we are on the same page with a target date."

"Both of those ideas sound great. If you think it's possible for me to work even faster, I am definitely looking forward to learning more about how."

7. Commit to Action

As you are doing mental backflips to celebrate making it through this conversation, do not forget to commemorate your success in writing with a few specific actions to take advantage of next.

If you personally were having a difficult time with say, giving presentations, and your manager engaged you in a Transformational Conversation that ended by asking you to present at the company's thousand-attendee annual meeting, would you feel excited or more like losing your lunch on her shoes?

The key is to keep your employees on the more excited end of the spectrum. You can elicit excitement by combining small, progressive actions with total support and continuous coaching. Your action items together should resemble putting a jigsaw puzzle together one piece at a time, with you there guiding the employees and supporting their success.

We typically recommend committing to only one to three small actions at the end of the conversation. The actions should be specific and align with the accountability process:

    a. A clear understanding and individual ownership of commitments made

    b. A disciplined system of check-ins and reporting

    c. The team and individual ability to hold others responsible for their actions and coach them to success

Once you've established clear understanding and individual ownership of commitments made, be sure to schedule a check-in within one or two weeks to review progress. Offer truthful, specific, timely feedback as appropriate. You have now combined powerful, motivating coaching with clear accountability.

The employee's performance can go one of two ways. With the newly found clarity and specific guidance, it may begin to improve, or it won't. We've seen performance reach new heights after one of these conversations, and we've seen it remain stalled. The latter case required additional conversations and sometimes performance improvement plans. Either way, you have navigated seemingly treacherous waters to offer support in an emotionally intelligent way. You created space for your direct report's emotions and needs, which may have felt nerve-wracking since despite immense preparation on your part, you were not in control. But isn't that the point? Being emotionally intelligent does not mean always being in control. It means having the tools to perform masterfully as a leader in any situation, given any variables. After all, isn't that why you picked up this book in the first place?

The Transformational Conversation is a tool that takes time to master. During at least the first few conversations, you will want to ensure that each step of the conversation is prepared and included. Once you feel comfortable with the individual pieces, you will most likely notice yourself engaging in more meaningful conversations on a regular basis, leveraging the pieces individually outside of high-stakes discussions.

The Powerful Tool You Didn't Know You Were Missing

Many leaders we have worked with find that the Transformational Conversation is the missing coaching tool they needed to feel truly confident in their skills. Because they felt uncomfortable engaging in dialogue about topics loaded with emotion, their accountability and coaching skills never reached as far as they could, and therefore their team's performance didn't either. This sometimes left the leaders feeling powerless and even resentful. With a formula for exploring problems deeply and compassionately, the leaders were able to balance complete forthrightness with care and respect for their direct reports.

Learning how to handle the most difficult conversations with ease means you are prepared to manage the everyday give-and-take of relationships skillfully. In terms of the spectrum of emotional intelligence, the Transformational Conversation requires the leader to leverage skills from each of the five levels at once, a challenging practice that builds and embeds emotional intelligence for life.

A Final Note on Coaching

We've covered a lot of ground. From purpose and values to key performance indicators, individual development plans, and the Transformational Conversation, you've picked up a lot of tools for your performance improvement toolbox. At the heart of this book, however, is a very simple concept: You are your team's coach, and your team members rely on you to identify the specific ways the team can improve to reach new heights of success. By adopting a coaching mindset and practice, you unleash your team's potential while making your leadership very attractive to a future pipeline of top talent.

Every framework and best practice included on these pages helps you further define what your team stands for. Without a clear understanding of identity and expectations, none of your team members can reach their fullest potential. Whether you are a CEO or a midlevel manager, each of the practices listed in this book is within your abilities for bridging current performance to best performance.

Coaching and accountability become infinitely easier once a team knows what they are working toward, what their roles are, and how the rules of the game are defined. By offering the utmost clarity on purpose, values, competitive advantage, and clear ownership of commitments, you place your team and yourself in a position for coaching success.

You will make mistakes, and you will sometimes wish a coaching conversation went a bit differently. And, just like your direct reports, you will continue to build your leadership skills through intentional practice and reflection. In our years of leadership and consulting experience, we observed that the leaders who combined intention with discipline year in and year out were rewarded with growing influence, exciting new opportunities, and management ease. We know that once you start taking the first steps toward building the bridge to a higher performing team, you will grow in the confidence that you can lead your team far beyond the results you thought was possible. Don't wait, and don't let the status quo hold back your own growth and greatness. Pick one step from this book right now, and commit to applying it *this week*!

Endnotes

[1] Malcolm Gladwell, *Outliers: The Story of Success* (New York: Little, Brown, and Company, 2008), 47-50.

[2] John Kotter, *Leading Change* (Boston: Harvard Business School Press, 1996), 22-24.

[3] Jeffrey Schwartz, Pablo Gaito, and Doug Lennick, "That's the Way We (Used to) Do Things Around Here," *Strategy Business*, March 1, 2011, 5.

[4] Ibid., 6.

[5] Kotter, *Leading Change*, 38.

[6] Ibid., 71.

[7] Jeffrey Pfeffer and Robert I. Sutton, *The Knowing-Doing Gap: How Smart Companies Turn Knowledge into Action* (Boston: Harvard Business School Press, 2000), 7.

[8] David Fine, Maia Hansen, and Stefan Roggenhofer, "From Lean to Lasting: Making Operational Improvements Stick," *McKinsey Quarterly*, November 1, 2008.

[9] David Leonard and Claude Coltea, "Most Change Initiatives Fail—But They Don't Have To; Successful Change Initiatives Depend on Front-Line Managers—Not 'Change' Managers," *Gallup Business Journal*, May 24, 2013, 1.

[10] Pfeffer and Sutton, *The Knowing-Doing Gap, 77.*

[11] Rajendra Sisodia and David B. Wolfe, *Firms of Endearment: How World-Class Companies Profit from Passion and Purpose* (Upper Saddle River: Wharton School, 2007), 16.

[12] Ibid.

[13] The Work Foundation, *Cracking the Performance Code: How Firms Succeed* (London: The Work Foundation, 2005), 6.

[14] Ibid., 29.

[15] Christopher Niemiec, Richard Ryan, and Edward Deci, "The Path Taken: Consequences of Attaining Intrinsic and Extrinsic Aspirations in Post-College Life," *Journal of Research in Personality* 73, no. 3 (2008): 291. doi:10.1016/j.jrp.2008.09.001

[16] Niemiec, Ryan, and Deci, "The Path Taken," 291-306.

[17] Ibid., 304.

[18] Daniel Pink, *Drive: The Surprising Truth About What Motivates Us* (New York: Riverhead Books, 2009), 27-28.

[19] Ibid., 27-28.

[20] Douglas Ready, Linda Hill, and Robert Thomas, "Building a Game-Changing Talent Strategy," *Harvard Business Review*, January-February, 2014.

[21] "Deloitte Survey: Executives and Employees Believe U.S. Businesses Are Falling Short on Delivering Positive and Meaningful Societal Impact," accessed September 21, 2013, http://www.prnewswire.com/news-releases/deloitte-survey-executives-and-employees-believe-us-businesses-are-falling-short-on-delivering-positive-and-meaningful-societal-impact-207690261.html.

[22] Michael Porter, "What Is Strategy? (Competitive Strategy Analysis)," *Harvard Business Review*, November 1, 1996, 62.

[23] Doug Stayman, "How to Write Market Positioning Statements," *ECornell Blog*, March 20, 2015, accessed January 4, 2016, http://blog.ecornell.com/how-to-write-market-positioning-statements/.

[24] Sisodia and Wolfe, *Firms of Endearment*, 200.

[25] Paul Spiegelman, "Business Values Lead to Profits? Let's Prove It," *Inc.com,* July 11, 2012, accessed February 4, 2015, http://www.inc.com/paul-spiegelman/business-values-lead-to-profits-lets-prove-it.html.

[26] Bud Bilanich, *Leading With Values: 8 Common-Sense Leadership Strategies for Bringing Organizational Values to Life* (Dallas: Walk the Talk, 2004), 23.

[27] "Live The Core Values | About.zappos.com," accessed March 4, 2014, http://about.zappos.com/jobs/why-work-zappos/core-values.

[28] Tony Hsieh, "How Zappos Infuses Culture Using Core Values," *Harvard Business Review*, May 24, 2010, https://hbr.org/2010/05/how-zappos-infuses-culture-using-core-values.

[29] Wendy Boswell, John Bingham, and Alexander Colvin, "Aligning Employees Through 'line of Sight,'" *Business Horizons*, 2006, 500.

[30] Ibid.

[31] Ibid., 503.

[32] "Human Capital Management Strategic Alignment," *U.S. Office of Personnel Management*, accessed October 8, 2014, https://www.opm.gov/policy-data-oversight/human-capital-management/strategic-alignment/.

[33] Boswell, Bingham, and Colvin, "Aligning Employees," 506.

[34] Donna Parrey and Kevin Martin, "Performance Improvement in High-Performance Organizations," (Seattle: Institute for Corporate Productivity, 2013), 20.

[35] Parrey and Martin, "Performance Improvement," 20.

[36] Wendy Boswell and John Boudreau, "Employee Line of Sight to the Organization's Strategic Objectives-What It Is, How It Can Be Enhanced, and What It Makes Happen," *CAHRS Working Paper* 39, no. 10 (2001): 4.

[37] Marshall Goldsmith and Mark Reiter, *What Got You Here Won't Get You There: How Successful People Become Even More Successful* (New York: Hachette Books, 2007).

38 Dean R. Spitzer, *Transforming Performance Measurement: Rethinking the Way We Measure and Drive Organizational Success* (New York: American Management Association, 2007), 35.

39 Robert Kaplan and David Norton, "The Balanced Scorecard-Measures That Drive Performance," *Harvard Business Review*, 1992.

40 Parrey and Martin, "Performance Improvement," 23.

41 Jane Nelsen and Cheryl Erwin, *Positive Discipline: The First Three Years: From Infant to Toddler— Laying the Foundation for Raising a Capable, Confident Child* (New York: Three Rivers Press, 2007), 72.

42 Elaine Pulakos and Ryan O'Leary, "Why Is Performance Management Broken?" *Industrial and Organizational Psychology*, 2011 4, no. 2: 147.

43 Josh Bersin, "Are Performance Appraisals Doomed?" LinkedIn, November 2, 2013, accessed November 10, 2013, https://www.linkedin.com/pulse/20131102214028-131079-are-performance-appraisals-doomed.

44 Corporate Leadership Council, "Building the High Performance Workforce," (Washington, DC: Corporate Leadership Council, 2002), 74.

45 Amy Edmondson, Richard Bohmer, and Gary Pisano, "Speeding Up Team Learning," *Harvard Business Review*, October 1, 2001, 1.

46 Ibid, 4.

47 Sadie Dingfelder, "Solutions to Resolution Dilution," *Monitor on Psychology* 35, no. 1 (2004): 34.

48 Corporate Leadership Council, "Building The High Performance Workforce," 75.

49 Pulakos and O'Leary, "Why Is Performance Management Broken?," 157.

50 Ibid., 158.

51 Jeremy Dean, *Making Habits, Breaking Habits: Why We Do Things, Why We Don't, and How to Make Any Change Stick* (Boston: Da Capo Lifelong Books, 2013), 143.

52 Elaine Pulakos, *Performance Management: A Roadmap for Developing, Implementing, and Evaluating Performance Management Systems* (Virginia: SHRM Foundation, 2004), 4.

53 Gabrielle Oettingen, "The Problem With Positive Thinking," *New York Times*, accessed October 24, 2014.

54 Joris Luijke, "Atlassian's Big Experiment With Performance Reviews," *Management Innovation Exchange*, January 16, 2011, accessed January 6, 2016, http://www.managementexchange.com/story/atlassians-big-experiment-performance-reviews.

55 Will Felps, Terence Mitchell, and Eliza Byington, "How, When, and Why Bad Apples Spoil the Barrel: Negative Group Members and Dysfunctional Groups," *Research in Organizational Behavior* 27, (2006): 178.

56 Felps, Mitchell, and Byington, "How, When, and Why," 191.

57 Ibid., 192.

58 Susan Scott, *Fierce Conversations: Achieving Success at Work & In Life, One Conversation at a Time* (New York: Viking, 2002), 20.

59 Headquarters Department of the Army, *A Leader's Guide to After-Action Reviews* (Washington, DC: Headquarters Department of the Army, 1993), 1.

60 Jon Hoffman, ed., *A History of Innovation: U.S. Army Adaptation in War and Peace* (Washington DC: Center of Military History, 2009).

61 Steve Crabtree, "Worldwide, 13% of Employees Are Engaged at Work," *Gallup.com*, October 8, 2013, accessed January 6, 2013, http://www.gallup.com/poll/165269/worldwide-employees-engaged-work.aspx.

[62] Marco della Cava, "Benioff: USA Needs 'Compassionate Capitalism,'" *USA Today*, accessed April 4, 2015.

[63] Daniel Goleman, *Emotional Intelligence* (New York: Bantam Books, 1995), 42.

[64] Ibid.

[65] Travis Bradberry and Jean Greaves, *Emotional Intelligence 2.0* (San Diego: TalentSmart, 2009), 21.

[66] Jonathan Haidt, *The Happiness Hypothesis: Finding Modern Truth in Ancient Wisdom* (New York: Basic Books, 2006), 4.

[67] Bradberry and Greaves, *Emotional Intelligence 2.0*, 17.

[68] Goleman, *Emotional Intelligence*, 16.

[69] Ibid., 213.

[70] Ibid.

[71] Ibid., 22.

[72] Scott, *Fierce Conversations,* 218.